I0840960

Ready player one - the movie: Raiders of the easter eggs
Unofficial Guide

Giuseppe Benincasa

&

Vittorio Canepa

TO

We dedicate this work to all those who, like us, have lived a happy childhood in the 80s and 90s. May your minds and hearts rejoice once again.

.

Sommario

Thank You

It is our pleasure to thank all those who directly or indirectly contributed to realize our dream. Thanks to Andrea Guglielmino for the support and for his valuable advice. Thanks to Franco Benincasa, Valerio Sorrentino and Fabio Capizzi for their suggestions and their interest. Thanks to Roby Rani and the guys of his Facebook group Italian Gunter Clan for some tips and finally we thank Ernest Cline and the master Steven Spielberg for making us go back to living the eighties, to what we were, with joy and a touch of melancholy.

Giuseppe Benincasa & Vittorio Canepa

Preface by Pauline Barrett

Thanks to my job, I have been working on video games for years, and partly in cinema. When I think back to the '80s, those carefree and imaginative moments that have characterized them come to mind. Watching a movie like Ready Palyer One could not help but get excited.

Seeing and reviewing the movie, however, I felt that something was missing. Something that really completes the movie. Well, thanks to this book I finally completed the puzzle. I found the missing pieces that allowed me to perceive each scene and understand the tributes that Steven Spielberg and his team put in Ready Player One.

The in-depth study that the authors of this book have made on every single frame of the movie has brought to light elements that have long been buried in my memory.

Thanks to them, I dusted off my set of AD & D and the legendary Commodore 64, which incredibly still works. In addition, the book highlighted new elements of those years that I missed, and that I was careful to recover.

While reading this book I realized that it is not a sterile list, but a real journey through the history of the '80s and' 90s.

Introduction
Ready Player One – Revenge of the Nerds

"Nothing new gets invented anymore" could be one of the most recurrent phrases in the world of art. And from quite some time, knowing how to remake something that was good in the past, possibly reinventing it, has become an art itself.

Ready Player One comes to the theatres as a movie adaptation from a book of the same name by Ernest Cline. Born in 1972, he could arrange a simple tale with lots of references to the world of entertainment (videogames, movies, TV series, toys, etc.) which characterised his adolescence, as well as that of those born in the '70s and '80s. Fruitful years where tech wizards, movie directors (including Steven Spielberg) and various artists gave their contribution to build a world of pop culture with solid foundations, resistant against the flow of time.

From those wondrous years that were the '80s, pop culture enthusiasts called nerds were born. They have been also known as geeks, depending on the attitude or behaviour they have towards the "outside world". For convenience, we will use the term nerd to include the (complex) idea of enthusiasts and followers of the pop culture. We should mention that the term nerd was created to label negatively those people who were often clumsy or incapable of interacting with the "real world" because of too much study, too many movies or too many videogames. The dividing line between said negative label and the modern meaning of this word can be identified in The Big Bang Theory, a TV series aired in America in 2007 that has nerds as stars.

This series' protagonists legitimised the term nerd for the big young audience of today, managing to create empathy with them and even a model for them to follow. The Big Bang Theory fired up a desire in young people to recover a past that did not belong to them. And in doing so, to make it theirs. This time not to close themselves in their rooms, but on the contrary to be integrated in a society where nerds' pop culture became mainstream. And where even while drinking in a pub (unthinkable pastime for a nerd of original concept), young people can chat about the latest episode of their favourite TV series. Of course,

Ready Player One's protagonist is a nerd (like the author) who knows perfectly the '80s, he makes quotes from them with his friends, he talks about them and he wears clothes from them. The idea of Ernest Cline's novel is to make a journey in his childhood's memories by engaging on a treasure hunt in a futuristic virtual world, definitely fascinating for whoever can be considered a videogamer. The movie with the same name by Steven Spielberg refers to the novel, adjusting it for the big screen by adding hundreds of references and quotes from the nerds' world.

The book you are holding in your hands (made for fun and written by nerds for nerds) will take you to the discovery of more than 800 quotes and references contained in the movie Ready Player One. We will proceed chronologically, dividing the movie by scenes, whereas at the end of this book you will find a list of quotes divided by category.

James Halliday a look back to look forward

James Halliday is the creator of OASIS, a place with no rules where everything is possible and everyone can be anything they most desire. Halliday was born in 1972 and dies in 2039 at the age of 67. He is a genuine nerd. An introvert who lives in his world made of videogames, movies and role play games. He finds difficult to approach women and he feels insecure in the "real world". His brilliance conceived OASIS. As its creator, he's loved and praised by nerds from all over the world and he's even compared to Steve Jobs.
But have you asked yourselves what James Halliday's true legacy is?
We know that whoever finds the easter egg will literally own OASIS, its servers, its stocks, and its future. But what does Halliday really want to leave to the next generation? The movie's message seems to be clear. Spend more time in the real world. Give more importance to human, concrete relationships. We interpreted the three tests built by Halliday as the three spirits visiting Ebenezer Scrooge during Christmas Eve. He was a man who clung to money, he did not cultivate relationships with anyone and he lived by himself without enjoying life. And yet, even Ebenezer Scrooge was young once, he had his chances, he had his love interests but he wasted it all. Halliday is almost like Jacob Marley. And we are wannabe Scrooges, entrapped in our homes searching for the best WiFi signal, glued to our chair, drinking carbonated drinks and lit by bigger, and bigger screens.

Halliday's life has been spent stuck to a screen. He never had the courage to do what it had to be done to live the love of his life, to raise his head towards the future. Holliday died with one of the biggest regrets that a man can have and, like Scrooge, he tells us that money does not give happiness. Life itself does.

First Challenge

During a debate in a bar, it's Halliday himself who tells his friend Ogden Morrow how good it would be to go back as fast as possible. To go back and change the past. To correct one's mistakes and not to have remorses anymore. Then Parzival runs backwards with his Delorean to pass the test..

Second Challenge

The Shining is the key-movie that represents the biggest regret in Halliday's life. He could not go beyond. He could not declare his love to Karen Underwood and he was not able to make that jump that later allows Art3mis to win the second key.

Third Challange

Lastly, the third test in which Parzival must play Adventure but he must not win or beat any records. He only has to have fun and find out what Warren Robinett left as signature in his game. So it's not about coming first before others. Instead, it's about to find out the meaning of things in their heart. In this case, of a game called Adventure (of life?).

Guide to reading

This book, born as a game and written by nerd for nerd, takes you to the discovery of over a thousand citations: easter egg and references contained in the movie Ready Player One.

Our research of the easter eggs, contained in Ready Player One directed by Steven Spielberg, goes hand in hand with the vision of the movie. Scene after scene, from the first minute, we try to show you all or almost all the citations and references contained in the movie so that you can cover it with this volume in hand.

This book is not supported by images, so we will be meticulous in pointing out the easter eggs, which we have scrupulously checked. The book is divided into chapters that correspond to scenes, places and characters in the movie. Sometimes we describe a character or a vehicle and this, for the sake of order and clarity, is described entirely the first time.

The characters to which we refer, of course, are to be considered avatars and not the "real" characters of the respective fantasy universes to which they refer.

We like to think of this book as an interactive guide, to be read and then reread in front of the screen. Cover the movie and find the easter egg that we have found by browsing 201296 frames, and maybe you will find new ones that you can report.

Have fun!

The Stacks

Our protagonist lives in the stacks. A place that looks like a landfill. Even before Wade leaves his home, we hear the **Jump** song by the American band *Van Halen*. The single, with the namesake title, was released in December 1983. The complete album, on the market a few months later, in which Jump is contained is titled "1984". Wade wears an **Eastpak backpack**, the same brand but different model, that uses Marty McFly (played by Michael J. Fox) in *Back to the Future*. 1985 cult movie directed by Robert Zemeckis. In the lower part of the backpack there is a patch of cloth with **three cubes**, this is reminiscent of the cubes that skips the character *Q * Bert* in the videogame of the same name, a 1982 platformer / puzzle created by Gottlieb. This video game appeared for the first time in a movie in 1984: Moscow on the Hudson (Moscow on the Hudson directed by Paul Mazursky) with Robin Williams.

Wade, on his wrist, has a **Casio CA-53W** watch that is the same one that Marty McFly wears in Back to the Future. The Casio CA-53W was one of the first calculator watches of the eighties.

The shoes are **Converse Chuck Taylor ALL STAR** model. The name of these shoes, since 1932, is signed to basketball player Charles Hollis "Chuck" Taylor. One of the drones delivers a pizza to one of the people living in the stacks. The pizza is contained in a box of the famous American chain **Pizza Hut**. The pizza, which a drone delivers to one of the condominiums, is from the famous American chain of pizzerias Pizza Hut. This reminds us of the character of

Space Balls, which in the original version is called Pizza The Hut. Space Balls is a movie directed by Mel Brooks in 1987 and is a parody of Star Wars. In the English version, while talking about a piano, from a billboard you hear the mythical phrase "no pain no gain", an expression by **Jane Fonda**. The actress in 1982 began to produce a series of videos about how to do aerobics at home. During these videos, it was customary to use this expression to push viewers to bear fatigue and muscle pain. The neighbor, with whom Wade talks, wears a **t-shirt** with a printed cover of the 1983 ***Syncronicity*** album, made by the English-born group The Police. Syncronicity is also their last album

Wade's van

The interior of Wade's van is furnished with lots of newspaper articles and cutouts that speak of James Halliday, and is full of cult objects and references to the '80s.

As soon as Wade enters the van, on the right there are **two stickers** of **_Garbage Pail Kids_**, published by Topps Company in 1985. In Italy they were published under the name of **Sgorbions** a few years later. They were trash figurines depicting scuffing to do something disgusting and insane. They were born to be a parody of the famous **Cabbage Patch Kids dolls**. These stickers were contained in the Chewing Gum packs, created by Art Spiegelman and Mark Newgarden.

The frame now focuses on the collar that is about to wear Wade. The collar hangs from a **Competition Pro Joystick** from **_Kempston Micro Electronics_**, built in the early 1980s. This object is attached to a wooden platform resting on the wall of the van. The joystick can be used on almost every console and home computer of the '80s and '90s.

In this frame we also note a **sticker** depicting a **_smile_**.

Just below the joystick there is a disassembled **Ipod**, produced by **_Apple_**. Below, we can see another **joystick**, the **_QuickShot Python 2B QS-197_** for Super Nintendo SNES, produced in 1992. On the small cabinet to the left of Wade there is glued a **sticker** that recalls the game of **_Q * Bert_**.

Wade takes off his glasses, and puts them on a branded **_Lunchbox Masters of the Universe_**. This box is a 1983 creation of Alladin. There are represented the characters of **He-Man, Skeletor, Teela** and hidden from the pack **Stratos**. In the side, which we see upside down, are depicted: **He-Man** on his trusty **Battlecat, Zodac** and **Man At-Arms** on the **Battle Ram** vehicle. This is a very famous series of toys (action figures for the most part) from the 80s produced by Mattel that marked an entire generation. The success of the Masters of the Universe line has given rise to the creation of cartoons, comics, movies, and video games. Even today, there are many collectors in the world and Mattel continues to reproduce the characters. Above the box there is a **pack** of ***Pop Rocks*** candies that have been produced since 1975 by General Foods. Near Wade's hand we can see a **Tootsie Roll bar,** a historic snack, for Americans, born in 1907 in Chicago. The **glove** that Wade wears is reminiscent of the 1989 ***Power Glove,*** made for Nintendo. Before being commercialized this device appeared as a "protagonist" in the movie The Little Great Wizard of Videogames (The Wizard - 1989), directed by Todd Holland.

The viewer Wade is wearing has some **stickers** on it. These include:

• **The Space Invaders** videogame **logo.** This video game is one of the most featured in the movie Ready Player One, it was produced by Taito in 1978, it is a fixed screen shooter.

• **Scratch 'n Sniff** sticker line produced by Trend. Marketed in the early 1980s, they were round, one-and-a-half-inch stickers with the Stinky Stickers brand. What you see on the viewer is **Peachy**'s character. The peculiarity of these adhesives is that they had their own perfume that can be found with the sense of smell.

• **A Red Revolution Fist** sticker produced by RedBubble.

Australian fashion and design company, founded in 2006.

• To the right of Wade is the **logo** of the 1982 *Joust* platform videogame from William Electronics, we will find this game later on.

• At the center of the display is the **logo** of the *Midway* videogame company. This company has made many iconic videogames including Mortal Kombat (which we will find later).

• Finally on the bottom left, there is a sticker representing the **Batman logo** in reference to the movie *Batman* (1989) directed by Tim Burton. The dark knight was played by Michael Keaton.

18

OASIS

OASIS stands for Ontologically Anthropocentric Sensory Immersive Simulation and it is an MMOSG that stands for massively multiplayer online simulation game.

To enter Wade must wear a visor and, of course, the first time he does so he must explain to the viewer what it is.

When you enter OASIS you decide in which world to go and cross a portal. During this first trip, Wade meets and shows us other **worlds**. The first is that of **Minecraft**, based on the game made by Notch in 2009. It follows the **Hurricane Hang Gliding** platform that allows players to fly with a hang glider. This is reminiscent of the action mode in the Nintendo 64 **PilotWing64** video game, developed by Nintendo in 1996.

Wade goes through a giant hurricane where a small country house hovers in the air. The scene recalls the movie Wizard of Oz. In the movie, the hurricane takes the house away, transporting it to a fantasy world. The movie is from 1939 and is directed by Victor Fleming and starring Judy Garland.

The **surf holiday planet**, on incredible waves, is reminiscent of the California Games videogame. Developed for Console and home computers in 1987 by Epyx.

Mount Everest, the highest in the world with its 8,848 meters, is climbed by **Batman** who has the appearance of Tim Burton's **Batman** in 1989 played by Michael Keaton. But, the style of his climbing is very similar to the one played by **Adam West** in the television series (1966), composed of three seasons

Planet Casino has the structure of the orbiting station of the movie: *A Space Odyssey in 2001*, directed by Stanley Kubrick. This structure represents a Casino that is also a reference to the space station of the animated series *Cowboys Bebob* (1998). The planet Casino is shown in the third episode of the series.

Entry in OASIS

After a blinding white light in full screen, we virtually enter a corridor and a large hall with countless characters. Among these, following the camera shot from left to right we have:

The huge **Cyclops** is identical to the one shown in the movie **The 7th Voyage of Sinbad** (1958), directed by Nathan H. Juran. Its peculiarity is that it is one of the creatures created by the stop motion master Ray Harryhausen. In the center, two cult characters from the Universe of Monsters created by Universal Pictures. In their original versions there are: The Wolf Man the monster of the homonym movie (1941) by George Waggner, and immediately behind it the **Frankenstein** monster of the homonym movie (1931)

 directed by James Whale, with Boris Karloff in the monster part.

The **girl** in a striped dress, transforms her avatar into *Flash* well known comic book character DC Comics, created by Gardner Fox in 1940.

Zitz and **Rush** who are characters from the console videogame *Battletoads*, developed by Rare in 1991. It is a game of slang fighting genre. This game is famous for its high difficulty. Continuing, it clearly distinguishes **Robocop** protagonist of the namesake cult movie by Paul Verhoeven (1987). The movies of Robocop are three, and there is also a remake (2014). In the American city of Detroit, where the movie is set, thanks to a kirkstarter campaign 67 thousand dollars have been collected. The money was used to build, a bronze reproduction of the 3 meter high robotic policeman. Following is the little **Marvin the Martian**, a cartoon character from Warner Bros. Marvin appeared for the first time in the episode of the Looney Toons animated series titled Devil of a Hare (Haredevil Hare), broadcast on July 24, 1948. On his left are four **Orendi** characters from *Battleborn*: first-person shooter game developed by Gearbox Software in 2016. Followed by the same game, the giant Shayne and Aurox.

After this roundup, and just made the acquaintance of Parzival, there are some characters in line that are about to enter some portals. In the lower portal of the screen we recognize the character of **Tracer**, protagonist of the video game *Overwatch*: developed by Blizzard Entertainment in 2016. It is a first-person shooter genre. Tracer was the hero character created by the developers to test the first versions of the video game. Alongside Tracer there is an **old woman** who remembers very much *Emma Webster*, the grandmother who holds Titty, the canary of the Warner Bros. cartoons called Looney Toons. Further back we see the **Catwoman** from the movie by Tim Burton *Batman Returns* 1992. In line there is also the legendary sprinter **Sonic the Hedgehog**, based on the homonym videogame developed by SEGA in 1991 for SEGA Master System. It is a video game of sliding platform genre. The first appearance of Sonic the Hedgehog did not happen in the videogame of the same name, but in the one entitled **Rad Mobile** (1991), always owned by SEGA. Rad Mobile is a driving simulation genre. When the shot crosses the line, **John Bender** stars in the movie *Breakfast Club*, John Hughes' 1985 cult movie in which actor Judd Nelson plays Bender. To the left of

Bender, **Nightwing** is noted in the version of the video game *Batman: Arkham City* (2011) developed by Rocksteady Studios. Nightwing appears in the character version playable in a DLC, his alter ego is Dick Grayson.

When the frame widens to move to the upper deck you can see, in a row in third position in the second portal, the avatar of **Wonder Woman** created by the psychologist William Moulton Marston and the designer Harry G. Peters in 1941. Among the characters not far from the portal, under the bridge, **Conan the barbarian** appears. The book that tells the story of Conan was written by Robert E. Haward in 1932, the cult movie version is represented by the movie titled **Conan: the barbarian** (1982), directed by John Milius.

Soon after, we follow the Avatar protagonist of Ready Player One on a bridge where **Hello Kitty** goes along with **Badtz-Maru** and **Keroppi**. These characters were created by designer Yuko Shimuzo and are part of the Hello Kitty fairytale world, which came to life in 1974. In 2007, UNICEF also assigned Hello Kitty a unique title called: UNICEF Special Friend of Children.

The being that we see from behind, on the bridge, with the mechanized arm is **Attikus** protagonist of the video game *Battleborn*. To the left of Parzival, from behind, we see passing the avatar of **Darryl "DMC" McDaniels**, one of the members of the American rap *group Run DMC* formed in 1981..

Doom Planet

To search for his friend Aech, Parzival visualizes in 3D an object made up of cubes, the **OASIS Sector Map**, this has the same features of the *Rubik's Cube* made up of 27 cubes. The Cube is a puzzle game, created by Ernő Rubik and commercialized in 1974.

Aech is on the planet Doom, a planet where deathmatch takes place, that is deadly combat. The term deathmatch, in video games, was used for the first time in 1983 by Drew Major and Kyle Powell during a session in the textual videogame Snipes. But in first-person shooters (FPS), it was used in the Doom videogame developed by id Software in 1993.

The name of the planet, **Doom**, is a reference to the homonym planet of the *Drule Empire* governed by King Zarkon in the series of cartoons *Voltron* aired between 1984 and 1985 with a total 124 of episodes total.

Among the characters on the planet, the first to be shown is the mecha scorpioni, a reference to the mecha **scorpion** of the videogame *Ultrabots* developed by Electronic Arts in 1993. In the video game there are three types of robots: humanoids, scorpions, and Scouts.
The bipedal creatures against which the mecha scorpions fight are the flying warrior ostriches of the arcade Joust.
Aech kills **Freddy Krueger**, protagonist of Wes Craven's horror movie *Nightmare*, which began in 1984. In this version Krueger has two gloves with blades and not just one

like in the original saga.

After the explosion, Freddy Krueger's avatar releases, among other things, a **Krieg's Buzz Ax**. This weapon is featured in the video game *Borderlands*, a first person shooter made by Telltale Games in 2009.

While in the trenches, Aech hits **Man-Bat**, an enemy of *Batman* who looks like an anthropomorphic bat. This character was created by Frank Robbins and Neal Adams in 1970. When he is about to leave the trenches, Aech strikes with his weapon a character that has the avatar of **Duke Nukem**, this is armed with a rocket launcher. Duke Nukem is the protagonist of the video game of the same name created by Apogee Software in 1991. The first videogame of the series is set in 1997.

To eliminate Duke Nukem, Aech uses an **MA5B Individual Combat Weapon System** assault rifle in the *Halo* video game series. Halo is a science-fiction shooter series created by Bungie in 2001. From this hit series have created comics, novels, and movies. Aech to continue the battle chooses a weapon particularly significant for fans of Arnold Schwarzenegger. It is an **EM-1 Railgun** that the character of John Kruger, played by the muscular Arnold, uses in the movie *Eraser* (1996) directed by Chuck Russell.

In the planet Doom we see Sho and Daito for the first time. Daito defeats **Scorpion**, *Mortal Kombat*'s videogames character. This game is a fighting game created by Midway Games in 1992. From the success of this series have been produced movies, comics, live action, and animation TV series. While Sho fights against the **Wolfman**, who is then shot down by Aech. Moreover, Aech hits with a precision shot **Deadshot**: a DC Comics character, an enemy of

Batman created by David Vern Reed in 1950.

Daito's face is inspired by that of the actor *Toshiro Mifune*. Mifune was an actor, movie producer, and Japanese director, probably the most famous of his country ever. He has acted in most of the Japanese director Akira Kurosawa's movies.

Among the characters struggling on the planet Doom we can see **Ryu** hurling his shōryūken and **Honda** fighting on the mountain. Both are characters from the *Street Fighter* videogame, a fighting game created in 1987 by Capcom. The game has been so successful that the videogame saga continues. Street Fighter can also count on a movie adaptation realized in 1994 written and directed by Steven E. de Souza with the participation of Jean-Claude Van Damme. After seeing Ryu and before seeing Honda, on the right of the screen we can see two **skeletons** climbing up. These are a tribute to the master of stop motion Ray Harryhausen who created warrior skeletons, which thanks to the stop motion technique interacted with real actors. Ready Player One presents a large number of skeletons that in some cases could also be a reference to the movie *The Army of Darkness* by Sam Raimi, a 1992 movie that concludes the Evil Dead trilogy.

The camera follows **Chun Lin**, a *Street Fighter* character to whom they also dedicated a movie in 2009 entitled Street Fighter la Leggenda. Chun Lin jumps to cling to the legs of **Commander Shepard**, this is the protagonist of the trilogy of Bioware's 2007 video game *Mass Effect*.

After the blaze coming out of the dragon's mouth we see Rick's avatar, Wade's aunt's boyfriend, and Jim **Raynor** with a cigar. Raynor is one of the main characters in the *StarCraft* videogame. Real-time strategy genre game, made by Blizzard Entertainment in 1998. StarCraft was an easter egg hidden in the video game Warcraft III: Reign of Chaos.

In the room in the real world of the defeated little girl screaming and throwing the viewer we can see, on the wall, a **poster** of **_Donkey Kong Junior._** This is a video game made by Nintendo in 1982, genre fixed-screen platformer. This is the first videogame that sees Mario in the villain part. Behind the little girl there is a **poster** that reproduces the cover of the album **_All lover the place_** (1984) of the female group **The Bangles**; next to it is the poster of **_Cyndi Lauper's_** _Shep's Unusual_ 1983 LP. On the bed there are **two teddy bears stuffed**, the blue one is part of the line of the bears of the **_Care bears_**, a series of characters created by American Greetings in 1981, as subjects for greeting cards. These are teddy bears, colored with pastel hues, each of which has a different symbol on the chest. In 1985 they debuted in a successful animated series and in two movies. A series of Care bears, in the action figure version, can also be found on one of the shelves, the third from above, to the left of the child. The Care bears were produced by Kenner. Sho and Daito eliminate an **avatar** with the features of **_Jason Voorhees_** protagonist of the horror movie saga of Friday the 13th (Friday 13th). The first episode was directed by Sean S. Cunningham in 1980. Freddy Kruger and Jason Voorhees are characters that belong to the same universe. In 2003, fans were able to enjoy watching the horror movie Freddy Vs. Jason directed by Ronny Yu who saw them both as protagonists.

Return to OASIS, the pre-race.

Let's go back to Parzival who walks and announces to his friend Aech that they are just ten minutes away from the race to get the first key.

On his right is the ninja turtle **Raphael** whose band is red. Behind it is **Leonardo**, a ninja turtle whose color is blue. ***Teenage Mutant Ninja Turtles*** are represented in their latest movie version. This is the reboot that counts two movies produced by Michael Bay. The first movie was released to the cinema in 2014, the sequel in 2016. The ninja turtles, protagonists initially of the comics created by Kevin Eastman and Peter Laird in 1984, have had several performances such as animated television series, video games, and live action movies as well as toys.

Also on the right of Parzival, **Dr. Emmet Brown** passes the nickname Doc in the saga of ***Back to the Future***. On this occasion he is represented with the yellow coat, the red shirt and the extravagant metallic glasses. Clothing that according to the director would have represented the one (2015).

Behind Parzival there is an avatar with wings, it is the character of **Benedict** of the video game ***Battleborn***. Finally, let's review the character of Conan the Barbarian in the background, in a central line compared to Parzival.

Introduce OASIS

OASIS was launched in 2025, and Halliday died on January 7, 2040.

During the presentation of OASIS, we see for the first time James Halliday with the blue jacket to which he seems very fond as he wears it in the three important moments of the movie: the presentation of OASIS, face to face with his friend Morrow in the company bar, and at the end when he leaves his legacy at Wade. This jacket has attached above **three pins**. From bottom to top are: one representing a ***20-sided die*** typical of the role-playing game Dungeons & Dragons, fantasy role-playing game created by Gary Gygax and Dave Arneson, first published in January 1974 by Tactical Studies Rules (TSR). Dungeons & Dragons (D & D) had its greatest success in the '80s, but it has always been played by nerds from around the world who have seen it grow and change, be trained in magazines, board games, video games, and even movie. The pin, to the left of the other two, represents the electronic game ***Simon***, very present in the life of James Halliday. The Simon game was created by Milton Bradley in 1978. Invented by Ralph Baer (creator of the first videogame console, the 1972 Magnavox Odyssey) together with Howard J. Morrison.

The pin higher up is a hidden quote for ***Ghostbusters***, in fact the pin has the inscription "I AM THE KEYMASTER", quote of a phrase of the character played by Rick Moranis (Louis Tully). Ghostbusters is a 1984 movie directed by Ivan Reitman and scripted by Dan Aykroyd and

Harold Ramis. The movie was one of the first blockbusters in the history of cinema in terms of budget. It is a horror comedy that is a cult, has several cartoon transpositions, a movie sequel, and a reboot (2016). Ghostbusters is still a very popular franchise whose toys are still produced.

In the OASIS presentation room on the far right and on the extreme left, two framed **posters** can be glimpsed. The one on the far left of Halliday is from the video game *Castelvania*; it is a series of videogames created by Konami, started in 1986. The series has more than 20 episodes playable on multiple platforms, and in 2017 Netflix produced the animated series.

The poster on the far right of Halliday is from the videogame *Gradius II*, a horizontal scrolling shooter, produced by Konami in 1988. It is the second chapter of the famous Gradius saga.

Halliday's death

James Halliday is virtually depicted in a coffin with 25 cents dollar coins, minted in 1972, on the eyes.

A **25 cents** coin in the eighties, in America, was used to play a game of an arcade video game; while 1972 is the year of birth of the author of the book, from which the movie is based, Ernest Cline. The year of birth of Halliday instead is 1973 as confirmed in an official document published on the site, made by the production of the movie.

The coins were placed on the deceased because, according to belief, they were used to pay **Charon**, who ferried the souls of the dead from one shore to the other of the river Acheron. If the dead were not given the coins, they could not take advantage of the favor of Charon, so they were forced to wander forever in the mists of the river.

The altar where Halliday's coffin is stationed is the **Star Trek theme.**

The **coffin** is identical to the one in which lies the lifeless body of Spock's character, played by Leonard Nimoy, seen in the movie ***Star Trek II: The Wrath of Khan*** (1982) directed by Nicholas Meyer . There is also the inscription "Mark VI" just like that of the movie Star Trek II: the wrath of Khan, and the blue and white flag.

Among the **crowns of flowers**, there is the reproduction of a starship ***USS Enterprise***, taken from the television series / movie **Star Trek. The USS** abbreviation means United Star Ship.

Star Trek was born as a television series in 1966 conceived

by Gene Roddenberry. The success was such that the television series of spin-offs and cinematographic works that continue to this day have been followed.

The **window**, on the bottom, and the other flower crowns reproduce the symbol of the **Starflleet Command. Starfleet Command** was born as a computer video game created by Interplay Entertainment in 1999, a kind of space and strategic flight simulation. This video game is based on the board game, the Starflleet Command Battles wargame created in 1979 which is based, in turn, and in an unofficial manner, to Star Trek. Finally, the three wreaths of flowers under the coffin represent the initials of the name of James Donovan Halliday.

When Halliday gets up, he has in his hands an object resting on the coffin. It is a **portable videogame** and precisely the ***Tomytronics Pac-Man Mini Arcade Handheld*** made in 1981. Finally Halliday shows **a T-shirt** with the logo of the game ***Joust.***

On Halliday's jacket there are the same three pins that we saw on the jacket in the presentation of OASIS. In this case they are placed differently.

The latest message from Halliday is disseminated online on all devices in the world. While announcing the hunt for the beast, one can see that one of the boys in the school, the one that has a sliding gate monitor, is wearing a **T-shirt** that has printed the ***Pac-Man labyrinth.*** Videogame designed by Toru Iwatani and produced by Namco in 1980. The game requires eating all the pills scattered in a labyrinth without being "eaten" by ghosts. This iconic game also had an animated version, broadcasted in the United States, from 1982 to 1984. Pac-Man also titled the musical album made by Buckner & Garcia in 1982. From 1981 to 1985 the Arlington Games Park in Texas had an area called Pac-Man land. The football player Adam Bernard Jones gave himself the nickname of Pacman Jones. Finally, Pac-Man is mentioned in several movies, has a key role in the movie Pixels (2015), and is used in plain sight in the movie Marvel Studios directed by James Gunn Guardians of the Galaxy Vol. 2.

34

Who is Parzival?

Before entering the portal, which will take him to the car race during his journey, Parzival passes next to a big-breasted man with a golden armor. This is **El Dragon**, a character in the ***Battleborn*** videogame.

Parzival is the avatar of Wade Watts, and we see it for the first time in the first roundup of characters related to OASIS.

We begin by knowing the name. Parzival is the knight who can see the Holy Grail. This relic could correspond to the one to be found as a legendary object. It is important to note that Wade chooses Parzival and not Parcival as the avatar's name. The character of the Arthurian cycle, known as Parcival, has an almost homonymous, Parzival, in the medieval epic poem attributed to the German poet Wolfram von Eschenbach. In this work, King Amfortas delivers the Grail castle. Just like Halliday who will deliver the reign of OASIS.

On the jacket he wears, on his back, is represented the **golden sword** in reference to the legendary ***Excalibur***. In its **belt** is the logo of the animated ***Thundercats*** series. This is a television series aired between 1985 and 1990. The protagonists are aliens with the feline form, from the series were made several comics and a video game.

The **brown belt** and the gun holster are like those of ***Han Solo***, protagonist of the Star Wars saga created by George Lucas.

The Race

To find the first key, the competitors have to face a race between what appear to be the streets of New York in the virtual world of OASIS, but which often turn into the **Hot Wheels** tracks. It is a line of toys that reproduces miniature tracks and vehicles. Born in 1968, this line of toys is still in vogue. It confirms an evergreen that has fans and collectors all over the globe.

We hear a very brief passage from the **song *I Hate Myself For Loving You*** by Joan Jett from 1988.

Parzival pilots a **DeLorean DMC 12** (1981) almost identical to that of the movie ***Back to the Future - Part II*** by Robert Zemeckis. The car of the second movie, in fact, has the hover function (the wheels fold to allow the flight). On the front of the car you can see a **LED** bar like of ***K.I.T.T.***, the car protagonist of the television series Knight Rider (1982). In the serial K.I.T.T. is a Pontiac Firebird Trans Am piloted by Michael Knight (David Hasselhoff) in the television series Supercar from 1982 to 1986. The car was equipped with artificial intelligence. The series was so much appreciated that it had sequels, TV movies, video games and board games. The world of pop culture has used, over the years, many quotations and references to K.I.T.T.

The dates that appear on the display of Parzival's De Lorean and which we will see during the race are, starting from low: **NOV (November) / 12/1955/06: 38** which is the date selected by Biff to return in 1955 from 2015, when he steals the Delorean in Back to the Future Part II.

FEB (February) / 11/2045/07: 27 the day and time when the race begins.

OCT (October) / 26/1985/09: 00 the date when Doc, Marty, and Jennifer return from 2015 in Back to the Future Part II.

Among the cars ready to go are: the **Batmobile** seen in the *Batman* television series (1966), led by **Batman** from the video game *Batman Arkham Asylum*. This car was created based on the 1955 Ford Lincoln Futura concept car.

The **A-Team van**. This is the same model used in the TV series with the same name which was aired from 1983 to 1987 or a GMC VANDURA (1983) appropriately modified. The series is about a group of veterans of the Vietnam war who, as outlaws, help the weak and needy people against ill-intentioned criminals and profiteers. The series has become a cult of the 80s.

A 1973 **Ford Falcon** (XB), the car that drives Max Rockatansky star of the post apocalyptic movie *Mad Max* directed by George Miller in 1981, whose saga continues today.

A red **Plymouth Fury** (1958). The same model and color of that protagonist of the horror movie *Christine* by John Carpenter (1983). To drive it, you will see during the race, there is **Dizzy Wallin** character of the videogame *Gears of War* made by Epic Games in 2007.

A red **Formula 1** car, later you will also see the green version. Reference to the 1981 Namole **Pole Position** videogame.

The Mach 5 driven by Daito is taken from the Japanese animated series *Mach Go! Go! Go!* (1967).

Sho leads a 1977 **Pontiac Firebird Trans Am**. This car is the protagonist of the movie with Burt Reynolds *The Smokey and The Bandit*, directed by Hal Needham in 1977.

During the race, for a brief moment, a 1980 **Ford LTD Country Squire Wagon Queen Family Truckster** appeared, starring in the tragicomic movie *National Lampoon's Vacation*, directed by Harold Ramis in 1983.

Art3mis, whose name is a reference to the Greek goddess of hunting, pilots the **motorcycle** of Kaneda protagonist of the manga and of the animated movie *Akira*, of Katsuhiro Ōtomo. Akira was born as a science fiction manga in 1982, adapted in 1988 in an animated movie directed by the same author. Akira is considered a masterpiece of its kind. On the bike there are several **stickers**: one of *Hello Kitty*, a sticker of the **Atari logo**, a US video game company founded by Nolan Bushnell and Ted Dabney in 1972. A **sticker** representing the *SEGA logo*, a japanese multinational founded in 1960 that produces video games. On the left side is the **logo Taito Corporation**, a Japanese videogame company, founded in Tokyo in 1953 by the Russian Michael Kogan. There is a **sticker** of *Ms. Pac-Man*. Ms Pac-Man is the protagonist of the namesake video game Namco (1980). On the right side there is a sticker with the **logo** of the television series *The Greatest American Hero*, which began in 1981.

In addition there is the **sticker** of the DC Comics *Wonder Woman* cartoon logo. Aech leads the legendary **Bigfoot** created in 1975 and appeared for the first time in 1979, is recognized as the first Monster Truck..

Among the participants in the race

Among the participants in the race there are:

Ryu character of the ***Street Fighter*** saga, you can see him walking among the cars. **Lara Croft**, heroine of the ***Tomb Raider*** video game series started in 1996 with the first chapter created by Core Design, relies on **Plymouth Fury**. It is an adventure and action game considered innovative. Comics and movies have been drawn from the videogame. Next to Lara Croft is **Dizzy Wallin**, a character in the ***Gears of War*** videogame.

Sub Zero, a character in the video game ***Mortal Kombat***, is seen near the back of Aech's Bigfoot. Shortly thereafter, Aech cites the movie by the Farrelly brothers ***There's Something About Mary*** in 1998, referring to Parzival's hair..

Ready player one - the movie: the raiders of the easter eggs

41

Oology Room

The members of the oology study the life of Halliday, and those we see work in the C7 sector. Every time we see them we will open a chapter for them.

The room consists of three desks:

The first desk has a **Colecovision**, a console marketed in 1982 and a **Nintendo Entertainment System** (NES). Specifically it is an 8-bit game console put on sale in 1983. The guy sitting on your left is watching, in the **monitor** in front of him, the first movie *Back to the Future*. Behind the girl sitting on your right, there is a **light panel** that reproduces a page of a *DC Comics* comic book. In the second desk the boy with glasses holds **two comics DC Comics**, the one in front is the comic *DC Presents vol.1 n. 76* of December 1984, starring Superman and Wonder Woman.

The third and largest desk has above three **Colecovision** and a **Nintendo Entertainment System** (NES) and a **SEGA Master System II** produced in 1990.

In the first screen that you see, the **red-haired boy** is looking at *E.T. The extraterrestrial*. Steven Spielberg's cult movie (1982). In the light panel there is a page of a **comic DC Comics** with *Wonder Girls* protagonist. In the last monitor there is a **box** of *Kellogg's Froot Loops*, the image is repeated a second and smaller time. In the monitor in front of the bearded guy, a *Cap'n Crunch* cereal box is shown (and repeated in a smaller version).

At the back of the room you can see a large screen showing a **map** of the island of Manhattan. It is not a map of any kind, but it is the one surrounded by very high walls (green) shown in the movie *1997 Escape from New York*, from 1981 by John Carpenter..

The race begins

During the race, Aech destroys a car belonging to the IOI. This has on the bonnet a **QR code** that scanned takes you to the following site:

http://www.jointhequest.io/. The viral website shows videos and posters related to the movie Ready Player One. When Aech frames the Art3mis bike with its optical viewer, **"AKIRA"** is read in the upper right corner.

Against the participants a **Freightliner FLC 120 Truck** is hurled, this is the same vehicle used by Jack Burton (played by Kurt Russell) in **Big Trouble in Chinatown**, in 1986 directed by John Carpenter. Soon after, you can clearly see the sign of the historic **Ratner's restaurant.** This restaurant on the Lower East Side of New York City opened its doors in 1905 and closed in 2004. The restaurant has been the scene of several scenes in TV series such as *Mad Men* and *Naked City*, and in movies like **The French Connection** (1971) directed by William Friedkin and *Boiler Room* (2000) directed by Ben Younger. During the race they pass the **National Video Center**, a video production company opened in 1959 and closed in 2002. Among the many works in which we participated we mentioned one of the masterpieces with Dustin Hoffman, Tootsie (1982) directed by Sydney Pollack.

A cinema shows the movie **Jack Slater III** in programming. Jack Slater is the protagonist (played by Arnold Schwarzenegger) of the 1993 action comedy *Last Action Hero.* In fact, Jack Slater has never had any dedicated movies.

Amongst the streets of Chinatown, **T. Rex**, the protagonist of the movie *Jurassic Park* directed by Steven Spielberg, breaks in 1993. Jurassic Park continues its movie saga today. From the Empire State Building in New York it makes its mammoth entrance on the **King Kong** scene. The giant ape from the island of Skull Island is the protagonist of the 1933 black and white movie of the same name. King Kong has had other movie incarnations, among them the 2005 version of Peter Jackson, from which the movements were taken for this King Kong.

while king kong destroys everything, you can see the neon sign Silvercup. This is identical to the one where the final scene of the movie *Highlander* (1986) directed by Russell Mulcahy takes place.

The Batmobile, before being hit by Aech's Big Foot, brakes by emitting a recognizable sound in the *jingle of the 1966 Batman television* series, composed by Nelson Riddle.

While Art3mis skips the high above destroyed, you can see a **Delta City billboard**. Delta City is the city that should have been born from the ashes of old Detroit in the *Robocop* movie.

When Art3mis takes off his helmet, behind him there is a **billboard** on which it is written **"ACE Chemicals"**. This is the company that "indirectly" has made the *Joker*, Batman antagonist in the comics DC Comics universe. On the other hand, when Art3mis complains to Parzival for having been grabbed while trying to get over King Kong with the bike, in the background you can see a **billboard** with a woman by the sea kissed by the sun. The writing reads **"Come to the ... Caribbean"**, this is the same bill in the movie *They Live*, in 1988 directed by John Carpenter. The curiosity of this advertising is that in the original movie it hides a subliminal message: "Married and reproduced".

46

Aech's garage

Aech's garage is a den of memorabilia and famous vehicles. The most obvious, of which we also see the design plans on the table next to the box that contains the works of Aech, is **The Iron Giant** that Aech is finishing to assemble.

The Iron Giant is the protagonist of the 1999 animated movie of the same name (The Iron Giant), directed by Brad Bird.

In the original version of the movie the voice of the Iron Giant is of the actor Vin Diesel.

At the entrance, near the door, there is the famous **Pee-Wee Herman bicycle** that we see in the movie *Pee-wee's Big Adventure* (1985), directed by Tim Burton.

When Parzival is about to open the box, with the projects of his friend, against the background of the garage meanders we can see the **extra-vehicular Pod** of the *2001: A Space Odyssey*, movie directed by Stanley Kubrick in 1968. The movie is a milestone of the science fiction genre, recognized as a masterpiece of cinema. And then the camper **Winnebago Chieftain 33** (1986). Of this camper, in the garage, there is the modified version to travel in the space that appears in the movie *Space Balls*. The camper nicknamed the Eagle 5 space RV, in the movie, is led by Lone Starr (Bill Pullman).

The **exoskeleton** of the animated series *Exosquad* (1993) produced by Universal Animation Studio. The **ED-209** (Enforcement Droid Series 209), or the robotic biped protagonist of the movie *Robocop*. In the movie, the ED-

209 was animated in stop motion.

A 1961 ***Ferrari 250 GT California***, from the 1986 youth comedy ***Ferris Bueller's Day Off*** directed by John Hughes.

The Thunderfight that pilots Buck Rogers starring Gil Gerard in the science-fiction television series ***Buck Rogers in the 25th Century*** (1979), aired for two seasons and a total of 37 episodes.

The Swordfish II, in repair, which is the spaceship of the protagonist of the 1998 ***Cowboy Beebop*** anime.

Aech's Lunchbox

The **lunchbox** is branded *Fraggle Rock*. This was a television show that premiered in 1983. Show, created by Jim Henson, made for children with the protagonists of the puppets of the Muppet series. On the table next to the lunchbox is the **Iron Giant project**, and on the other side of the work table is the **Cowboy Beebop Swordfish II model**.

While Parzival is preparing to open the lunchbox, on its right in the background, you can see tires with attached **rim**, one of these belongs to the *Mach 5*. Behind him, between the stairs, there is the famous **cabin** of the TV series Doctor Who, the *Tardis*. This British series is one of the most long-lived in television history despite some interruptions. Started in 1963, and still on the air, it is a cult series that has fans all over the world.

The Aech lunchbox contains many models that are as many references to pop culture:

The **Galactica spacecraft** starred in the television series *Battlestar Galactica* created by Glen A. Larso, and aired in the US in 1978. From this series of cult they realized a movie and a reboot series that was enormously successful. Also from this series, in the lunchbox, there is the **Colonial Viper** space fighter.

The stellar **spaceship USS Sulaco class Conestoga** comes from the movie *Aliens*, directed by James Cameron in 1986. In the movie the spaceship was used for the transport of the Colonial Marines.

The **spaceship Valley Forge** protagonist of the movie **Silent Running** (1972). The name of the spaceship derives from the eponymous aircraft carrier used in Korea. And it is inside the aircraft carrier that many scenes of the movie Silent Running have been shot. This movie was the inspiration for George Lucas in making Star Wars. The Italian title was an adaptation of convenience to try to bring to the cinema the fans of the movie Stanley Kubrick 2001: A Space Odyssey, released four years earlier. Silent Running was also the inspiration for some designs of the Battlestar Galactica series (2004-2009) by Ronald D. Moore.

We do not see it, but the **flagship Harkonnens** is named but not seen. This spacecraft does not exist in the movie **Dune** (directed by David Lynch in 1984), but is present in the novel of the same name written by Frank Herbert. This may suggest that in 2045, when Ready Player One was held, Dune had a sequel. Among the nominees there is also the planet Arakkis, also belonging to Dune.

Questions and Answers between Art3mis and Parzival

While Aech repairs the motion of Art3mis, ruined during the race to try to take the first key, Art3mis tests Parzival's knowledge of the world of Hallyday.

The **video game** is *GoldenEye007* for Nintendo 64 console made by Rare in 1997. The preferred game mode, always in GoldenEye007, is "only slaps" (slappers), which is the most difficult mode of the game.

The favorite character is **Oddjob**. This is the villain of the movie **Agent 007: Mission Goldfinger** (1964), directed by Guy Hamilton. The villain is played by Harold Sakata. Oddjob, however, is not one of the main villain, but it is a stooge of the gold magnate Auric Goldfinger. Oddjob is a powerful and silent Korean whose weapon is his hat, equipped with blades that he manages to launch like a boomerang. The role of James Bond played Sean Connery. This movie, among those of 007, was the first to win an Oscar (best sound effects).

As a favorite *racing videogame* from Halliday, he was named *Turbo*, an arcade produced by SEGA in 1981.

The favorite **sneakers** are the *Hot Pockets*. These sneakers are similar to stuffed sandwiches to cook in the microwave, they were created by Chef America Inc. in 1983.

Chuck E. Cheese's favorite restaurant, this choice hides another easter egg since this American restaurant chain was founded by Nolan Bushnell in 1977, after co-founded Atari in 1972. There are also video games featuring the mascot of the catering chain. In addition, Chuck E. Cheese's was inspired by the horror movie Five Nights at Freddy's and his following.

Video Killed the Radio Star of The Buggles (1980) is the favorite **song** by Halliday, while the favorite **video** clip is *Take On Me* of the band 1985 A-Ha.

The favorite **quote** is taken from the 1978 movie *Superman* directed by Richard Donner. The phrase uttered by Lex Luthor addressing Miss Teschmaker is: " Some people can read War and Peace and come away thinking it's a simple adventure story. Others can read the ingredients on a chewing gum wrapper and unlock the secrets of the universe. "

In the garage you can almost hear the **song** *Just My Imagination* by The Temptations (1971).

While Parzival and Art3mis speak, behind them there are some **posters**. Among these we can distinguish those, starting from the left of Art3mis, the banner of the videogame *Joust*, the banner of the video game *Gorf*, an arcade shooter created by Midway Games in 1981, and adapted later for consoles and home computers. The video game poster *Gauntlet* in the version for NES made in 1987. The original version is an arcade of Atari Games (1985), the game is inspired by Dungeons & Dragons. The poster of the *Contra* videogame published in 1987 by Konami, who for his success had several sequels. The videogame of the videogame *Galaga*, arcade of the shooter genre made by Namco in 1981. Finally, on the extreme right at the top, there is the poster of *Robotron: 2084*, an arcade of a 1982 fixed-screen shooter genre made by Eugene Jarvis and Larry DeMar and published by William Electronics.

Art3mis before leaving the garage of Aech quotes Back to the future by calling Parzival "***McFly***".

After a few seconds Parzival goes away and we return to see Wade who, after the dispute between his aunt and his companion, reflects by telling us why his name and his surname have the same initials. His name is Wade Watts because according to his father this could sound like the name of a superhero, and he mentions **Peter Parker** (Spider-Man) and **Bruce Banner** (Hulk). This is the only Marvel reference of the whole movie.

When the aunt's partner hits him with the glove, we can see on this, at the height of his thumb, a **sticker** with the ***Batman logo*** taken from the movie by Tim Burton.

After the aunt talked to Wade, and left him sitting on the floor, behind him was a **device** for the Colecovision console. This is the ***Coleco Driving Well*** with which you could play the video game Turbo.

55

Halliday Journals

Before entering the building, you can hear *Faith* 1987 **song** by George Michael.

When Parzival enters there is a panoramic view that shows us the **scenography** with tables, chairs, stairs, railings and fluorescent lights identical to that seen in the cult movie *Breakfast Club*.

In the lower left part, sitting on a chair, there is *Hello Kitty*. Instead, on the opposite side, to the right of Parzival, you can see, sitting at the desk, an avatar that reminds us of an *Imperial soldier* in the Star Wars saga.

For the first time we see the curator who, as stated by the moviemakers of the movie's concept art, is inspired by a classic butler of old movies. On the table there is **a Boston KS Pencil Sharpener,** a **crank pencil sharpener** with 8 holes, therefore usable with different types of pencils. It is a historical manual pencil sharpener made by Boston Pencil Sharpener, founded back in 1899.

Behind the curator there are **nine cabinets** visible. On his right, starting from the left, there are videogames: *Pole Position, Asteroids*, created in 1979 by Atari. The Videogame is contained as an easter egg in the Agilent HP 54622D oscilloscope. To activate it, you must execute a particular sequence of commands. *Millipede*: 1982 video game of Atari, this is a sequel arcade game of the *Centipede* game. On the left of the curator there are: Pong: 1972 *Ping Pong* simulator made by Allan Alcorn and produced by Atari. *Missile Command*: 1980 arcade always Atari.

Tempest arcade shooter developed by Atari in 1981. **Ms. Pac-Man**, another copy of **Millipede**, Dig Dug arcade Namco (1982), another cabinet of **Missile Command** with beside another cabinet of **Ms. Pac-Man**, and finally an other **Asteroids**.

Attic - Halliday assembles his first gaming computer (1985)

Halliday in 1985 is assembling his first computer to play. On his left, on the floor near the window, there is a **mask** of *Tetsuwan Atomu* better known as Astroboy. It is a manga created by Osamu Tezuka in 1952. Astroboy also boasts of several animated TV series (anime) and feature movies, several videogames were also made. Above one of the boxes there is the **electronic game Speak & Spell** (arrived in Italy with the name of Grillo Parlante), whose first model was introduced on the market in 1978 by Texas Instruments. Three **cans** of *Pepsi* keep him company. On the sloping ceiling, to the right of Halliday, we can see the **poster** of the movie *Revenge of the Nerds*, a 1984 comedy directed by Jeff Kanew. Below there is a **poster** of the *Xevious* videogame, an arcade produced by Namco, designed by Masanobu Endō, and published in 1982.

Ready player one - the movie: the raiders of the easter eggs

James Halliday with Atari 2600 (1983)

The Curator and Parzival pass in front of the play room of the small Halliday, in 1983. Halliday is playing with an **Atari VCS 2600** console built in 1977. The **game** he is playing is the arcade *Defender* published in 1981 by Atari. The room is sprinkled with objects of those years. On the left side starting from the bottom there are: the **game** *Simon* and the game *Connect Four* by the authors Howard Wexler and Ned Strongin, published in the United States in 1974. More over, near Halliday, there is a toy reproduction of the **van** *A-Team*. Near the back of the van is the *Tomb of Horrors* **game module**, an advanced adventure for 1978 Dungeons & Dragons. This adventure is famous for its high difficulty, it is recommended for characters who have reached at least the tenth level. Above, continuing towards the TV, there is the toy **vehicle** *Thundercats Tank* with two characters inside. At the bottom there is the **Grayskull Castle** built by Mattel in 1982, the *He-man* **action figures** mounted on *Battle-Cat*, and the enemy *Skeletor*. All part of the Masters of the Universe universe. Lying on the floor is the **toy** *Robby The Robot*, protagonist of the 1956 science fiction movie The Forbidden Planet. The character of Robby has been so successful that he has been included in several movies and TV series. Among the videogames, on the carpet, there is the **box** of *Space Invaders* and its cartridge. Continuing on the right you can see the **toy** of *Marvin the Martian*, as well as three **VHS** of the sci-fi series *The Visitors* aired between 1983 and 1984. There is the **game**

Etch A Sketch invented by André Cassagnes and realized by Ohio Art Company at the end of the 50s. This magic slate also appeared in animated form in Toy Story, Pixar animated movie (1995). Among the **images** of the discs is that of the ***Rush 2112***, album (1976), the one of the **soundtrack** of the movie ***Wargames*** and ***New Traditionalists*** of the DEVO from 1981. There is also a ***Batman* action figure** from the Mego's World's Greatest Superheroes collection! Produced by MEGO from 1972 to 1983. Still further down, closer to the window, is the electronic **game *Merlin*** marketed by Parker Brothers in 1978. Near the feet of Batman is the portable **game *Simon Pocket game***. Next to the latter there is the ***Thundercats Lunch Box***. Before arriving in the cafeteria room, on the left of Parzival, the cabin of the ***video game Tempest*** stands out from a dark room.

Gregarious Games Office Party (2029)

In the interior of the Gregarious Games cafeteria, where an office party has just ended, Halliday wears a *Space Invaders* videogame **T-shirt**. On the shirt instead he has the three **pins** of which we have written previously. The cafeteria has four posters. The closest to the Curator is the **poster** of the *Black Tiger* videogame, by Capcom (1987). The genre platform hack and slash is also known by the name Black Dragon.

In the background, where there are two cleaners, we can see the poster of *Mortal Kombat*, the other closest to our protagonists is the Japanese poster of *The Legend of Zelda A Link to the Past* made by Nintendo for Super Nintendo Entertainment System in 1991. Behind Ogden Morrow is a **poster** of the *Galaga* videogame.

Halliday names the video game Asteroids.

When Wade understands how to win the first key, he takes off the viewer and review the interior of his van. At the far left of Wade is a *Garfield cat* **sticker**. This is the protagonist of the homonym comic strip created in 1978 by Jim Davis. The comic is so famous that TV series, movie movies and three animated feature movies were made, as well as a long series of video games.

Parzival win the first key

When Anorak rewards Parzival for getting the copper key he refers to him as **"young padawan"**. This expression was pronounced in *Star Wars The Phantom Menace* (1999), a movie directed by George Lucas that opens the prequel trilogy of the original saga.

Virtual Shop

The scene of Aech and Parzival who go shopping opens with the voice of Bruce Springsteen **singing** a piece of his 1985, *or Stand on it*. The song is present in the soundtrack of the comedy Ruthless People (1986), directed by the trio Zucker-Abrahams-Zucker.

Behind the two friends, in virtual version, there is the **Avatar Outfitters logo**, the font is the same as the 2008 blockbuster movie *Avatar* by James Cameron. And immediately, on their left is **Ryu**, from *Street Fighter*, in front of to which there is the screen of the video game for the choice of characters.

In the shot from the top where we see Aech and Parzival behind, after passing that short gallery, we can see on the left a **Borderlands stand**. Next to the **stand** of **Halo** where **weapons** are sold: *Assault Rifle MA5D* individual combat weapon system and *the M45 tactical shotgun.* On the opposite side we can admire the **Overwatch** stand where **Tracer**, one of the protagonists of the videogame, is represented. In addition, from Overwatch, the **Widow's Kiss weapon** is on sale. Later we notice a red writing dedicated to **Dungeons & Dragons**, the famous role-playing game.

The first purchase of Parzival is the **Holy Granada**.This item is a tribute to Holy Hand Grenade that can be seen in the movie *Monty Python and the Holy Grail* directed by Monty Python in 1975. A similar bomb can also be seen in the *Worms* **videogame** produced by Team 17 in 1995.

Parzival runs to the **Zemeckis Cube**, on the way there is the opportunity to buy an **add-on** from *Blizzard*, followed by the **add-on** of *Madball*, they are balls that depict a monstrous and / or disgusting face. This line of toys was created in the mid-80s and is still produced today. A videogame and comics were born from this toy. It follows the **Peltzer Peeler Juicer**, or the particular juicer invented for the movie *Gremlins*. The juicer is an invention of Randall Peltzer who is the father of the protagonist Billy. Gremlins is a 1984 movie, directed by Joe Dante, based on a screenplay by Chris Columbus. Steven Spielberg is the executive producer. Gremlins had a sequel and several transpositions for videogames. *The Chucky Doll* **add-on** follows. Chucky is a killer doll starring in the horror movie series that began in 1988 and continued with several sequels, reboots, comics and video games. There follows an **add-on** of the video game *Halo*, it is the **weapon** of the Covenant named *Type-25 Directed Energy Rifle*.

The second purchase of Parzival is the **Zemeckis Cube**. This object has two references: the first to *Rubik's Cube* and the second to the director of the **Back to the Future** Robert Zemeckis trilogy. While Parzival admires the X1 suit in the background there is the box where you can buy the **Wolf Man's avatar.** It can be seen in the typical pose he assumes when he is transforming from man to wolf

The first meeting between Sorrento and I-R0k

The avatar of Sorrento leaves the **Martian ship** of the movie Byron Haskin *War of the Worlds* (1953), of which Steven Spielberg has made a remake in 2005. His **avatar** is very similar to *Captain Sternn*, protagonist an episode of the 1981 animated movie *Heavy Metal* by Gerald Potterton.

I-R0k has a **face** with somatic features very similar to a *Klingonian*. These are aliens protagonists of the TV series and movies of Star Trek.

I-R0k bends down to get the pirate steampunk skull, at this moment we can see the **Perseo's gold shield**, protagonist of the movie *Clash of the Titans*, directed by Desmond Davis in 1981 and characterized by special effects in stop motion by Ray Harryhausen. On the right you can see the legendary **whip** of *Indiana Jones*, protagonist of the saga directed by Steven Spielberg. When I-R0k gets up, raises the skull of the steampunk pirate, this can bring to mind the famous theatrical scene of William Shakespeare's drama *Hamlet* raising the skull of Yorik.

When the box containing the Osuvox globe is framed, while Sorrento's avatar is opening it, we can notice the presence of the **M1911 gun** belonging to *Duke Nukem* (protagonist of the videogames Duke 64, Duke Nukem Forever). Near that there is the **weapon** of Buck Rogers, or the *Space Guns - BUCK ROGERS XZ-35 Rocket Pistol "wilma"*. The **box** containing the Osuvox is the same as the one that contained the Mogwai in the movie *Gremlins*.

Inside the Osuvox you see an **energetic object** that has the shape of a 20-sided die (***D-20***) fundamental in the D & D role play (Dungeons & Dragons). Before the two leave, I-R0k mentions that Sorrento goes straight to the center as if it bites a ***Tootsie Pops***. These are lollipops invented in 1931 by Lukas R. "Luke" Weisgram, an employee of The Sweets Company of America. The company, due to the enormous success of the lollipops, changed its name in 1969 to Tootsie Roll Industries. The first taste to which the lollipops were associated was chocolate, then all the others were made. The reference to the biting at the center and the owl refer to a spot of lollipops in which a child asked an owl how many licks it took to get to the center of the Tootsie Pops. As you can imagine, the little boys used to lick the lollipop without having the patience to lick it up to that point.

Comeback in the Wade's Van

In this scene Wade reads the clue that will lead him to the second key. Meanwhile the director gives us a rundown of newspaper sheets attached to the inside wall of the van. Along with these, there are sticky notes and sheets of paper written by Wade as clues / notes and also some covers of various magazines, some of these are existing, others invented for the occasion. The first framing on the wall shows the magazine **Columbus Independent Newspaper**, this is inspired by the *Columbus Monthly magazine* and underlines the place where Wade lives, that is Columbus, the capital of Ohio. Next door is the **Bloomberg Businessweek magazine cover**. This, actually existing, is a weekly magazine founded in 1929 and published in the U.S. which is about economics. Under this cover, we see a sheet of notes on which we read the mentions to **Metaverse**, a term coined by Neal Stephenson in *Snow Crash* in 1992. This is a cyberpunk science fiction book, described as a sort of virtual reality where it is represented in three dimensions through your avatar. **Star Trek, Middle Earth** or the **Middle Earth** created by J.R.R. Tolkien is the protagonist of several novels such as The Hobbit and The Lord of the Rings. **Vulcan** is the planet of the *Star Trek Universe* from where Spock's Vulcan character originates. Peon is a species of the **Oror** of the mmorpg videogame *World of Warcraft* (WOW). It is the most famous videogame of its kind that counts millions of active users all over the world. From WOW they created comics, board games, collectible card games, movies and toys. **Arrakis** is the home planet of the main setting for the stories related to the Dune cycle. **Magrathea** is one of the planets that is told in the *Universe of Galactic Guide for hitchhikers*. These stories are born in 1978 as a radio program, then bring you back into fiction. These are humorous stories of science fiction that became cult and from which they created comics, video games and a movie. Following is the word **Discworld**, or **Disco World**, it is an imaginary world created by Terry Pratchett that has given life to novels, comics, video games and animated movies. Following the word **Riverworld**, it is the *World of the River*, location for the science fiction novels of the eponymous cycle written by Philip José Farmer since 1971. Finally **Ringworld**, the *World Ring* location protagonist in science fiction novels, created by the writer Larry Niven since 1970 .

Later we note that one of Wade's notes shows the directions of the Halliday funeral scene, which we have written extensively about before. Scrolling, we see a print of an internet page, it is a news from the **BuzzFeed** website founded in the United States in 2006. There is the newspaper page with the title "Halliday: bigger than Jobs?" Obviously the reference is to the co-creator of Apple **Steve Jobs**. Next to this newspaper clipping there is a front page of **The Columbus Herald**, a historical newspaper in print since 1881, which reports the news of the corporate divorce between Halliday and Ogden. The sheet with the word OASIS, highlighted in yellow, shows a Wade note on one of the sectors of that universe. The drawing is the same as the virtual object seen at the beginning of the movie that represents the OASIS map. Also below is written **"For gamer like Everquest"**, *EverQuest* is a fantasy MMORPG published in 1999 developed by Verant Interactive and published by Sony Online Entertainment.

When framed Wade, behind him on the right, we see an **NES Zapper**, produced in 1985 by Nintendo. This is an optical gun that allows interaction with some video games for the Nintendo Entertainment System console. The version used in the movie is from the first series, in fact it is all gray. From the second series they turn gray and orange.

When you come back with the framing on the inside wall of the van, after the briefing of the obituary page dealing with the death of Karen Underwood Morrow, there is a list. At the top highlighted there is written **"Copper"** which is the reference to the first key, "Set in New York" refers to the location of the first race. Following is a list of movies: **Ghostbusters** (1984), **Big** (which is cut) (1988) directed by Penny Marshall starring a young Tom Hanks, **Mad Max**, **Cannonball Run** (1981) movie directed by Hal Needham who tells of a clandestine race in the United States of America, 1997: Escape from New York (1981), directed by John Carpenter and starring Kurt Russell in 1981, he wears the role of the cult character Jena Plissken, **King Kong**.

When we see Wade again, on the left side of the frame in the background we see a pair of **black dice** with white numbers hanging from the rearview mirror. These are the famous *Fuzzy Dice* (dice of peluches) that were put on the market in the 50s as good luck.

Among the magazine covers, there is also **Wired**, an American magazine founded in 1993. On the left side there is a sheet of paper written by John Hughes. This is probably a list of the director / writer's movies. We can only see the first one that is National Lampoon's Vacation of which **Hughes** is a writer. On the right side of Wired magazine there is a not very visible sheet entitled **Adventure**. These are the instructions to access the eggester of the game. These will be useful for conquering the third key.

Halliday Journals: Parzival returns as a hero

The **song** that accompanies this entry to the Halliday Journals is Blondie's ***One Way or Another***, recorded in 1978.

While Parzival makes its entrance, it goes out of the Journals **The Arkham Knight**, the super villain of the video game ***Batman: Arkham Knight***, created by Rocksteady Studios in 2013.

The first to recognize Parzival is the **avatar** of ***Beetlejuice*** (with a different hair), protagonist of the homonymous movie directed by Tim Burton in 1988. From the desk closest to them stands **Supergirl**, a comic book world DC Comics. This shown is the version of the fighting video game ***Injustice: Gods Among Us***. Supergirl in the comics was created by Otto Binder and Al Plastino in 1958.

Among the characters that flock and among those that surround Parzival there is a back, with chains on the wrists, the **Frankenstein** monster; going forward appears from behind the stairs **Dizzy Wallin**. During the snapshot of the selfie we can see next to Parzival the avatar of the characters of **Ambra** from the video game ***Battleborn***, **Jill Valentine** protagonist of the videogame ***Resident Evil 3: Nemesis*** created by Capcom in 1999. **Lara Croft**, protagonist of the video game ***Tomb Raider***, there is also **Darryl "DMC" McDaniels**, finally there is **Batgirl** comic book character DC Comics. Created by Bob Kane and Sheldon Moldoff in 1961. This version of the character is from the video game ***Batman: Arkham Knight***.

At one point he breaks into the Art3mis crowd with **_Goro_'s avatar**. This is the villain of the video game Mortal Kombat in 1992. When they are left alone, Art3mis makes the joke of the chestbuster **Chestbuster** taken from **_Alien_**, Ridley Scott movie (1979). The Alien saga is composed of several movies plus two spin-offs where the xenomorphic fights Predator.

Art3mis transforms Parzival into Superman's ego of Superman, or **Clark Kent**, providing him with suitable looks and glasses. Superman is one of DC Comics' leading figures created by Jerry Siegel and Joe Shuster and appeared for the first time in comics in 1933. As Clark Kent walks, **Miko** character from the video game **_Battleborn_** passes behind him. A few moments later, still behind Kent, there is **Benedict**, a character from the same videogame.

Halliday and Morrow at the Gregarious Games headquarters

When Art3mis and Parzival are in front of the chosen diary, Art3mis rips Parzival's disguise. The action is reminiscent of the tearing of the silicone masks in the films of the Mission Impossible saga, which began in 1996. A gesture that you see also later.

The newspaper scene takes place in 2025, Halliday and Morrow are working. The album of Billy Idol Do not stop (1981) is on the desk.

You can see also André Previn in Hollywood (1963). André Previn is a jazz pianist, musician, composer and conductor of German orchestra. Among his works there are several compositions of soundtracks for motion pictures. He is winner of four Oscars, including that (1964) for My Fair Lady.

On the other side of the window, outside the office, you see a poster, this is the Japanese version of the video game Metroids created by Nintendo (1986), for Nintendo Famicom console. During the scene, Kira is named as the protagonist of the 1982 film Dark Crystal directed by Frank Oz and Jim Henson.

Behind Art3mis e Parzival there is a cabinet of Joust inside a cafeteria called Happy Time.

The reference to Rosebud (Rosebud) by Parzival is for the movie Citizen Kane by Orson Welles (1941).

The Lair of Aech

From the overview of Aech's lair we can see on the right, in the direction of the turntable, a **poster** with the words *Save Ferris*, it is a band formed in 1995 in California, which plays the genre ska punk. Their name is a wanted reference to the movie Ferris Bueller's Day Off. On the right is the **poster** of the video game *Metroid* in Japanese version and still on the right four **stickers** related to the videogame *Space Invaders*. On the cabinet next to the turntable there is a **lava lamp,** a decorative design object invented in 1963 by Edward Craven Walker, the tha **hat** wearing Marty McFly *in Back to the Future Part II*, the white **guitar** is *the Gretsch White Falcon Gibson ES-335* by Chuck Berry. In the open box, in front of the electric guitar, there is the **VHS** of the movie Airplane (1980) by Zucker-Abrahams-Zucker, instead of the box, the first down is the *Batman* **VHS** by Tim Burton. At the center of the frame is a horizontal-level **Pac-Man cocktail** cabinet. At the bottom right there is a **basket** for *Pac-Man* branded paper, on the left instead, on the floor behind the chair, there is a **VHS** of the movie *Labyrinth*, a **magazine** *A.N.A.L.O.G.* and the **VHS** by *E.T. The extraterrestrial.* To the left at the top of the frame is the **neon** sign "Cocktail & Dreams" featured in the movie *Cocktail* directed by Roger Donaldson, and starring Tom Cruise in 1988. Below is the **poster** of the movie The *Dark Crystal* and below still there is a **keyboard,** is *The Emulator II* and was made by E-mu Systems in 1984. The head of the missile that breaks through the floor is a reproduction of the **missile** that materializes, moving from a plane to the more inside Wyatt's house in the movie ***Weird Science*** (1985) directed by John Hughes

Sparse, and accumulated around the room, there are **magazines** of the magazine ***A.N.A.L.O.G. Computing*** (Atari Newsletter And Lots Of Games). The magazine was published in America and was dedicated to the Atari 8-bit home computer line, published from 1981 to 1989. And, there are also, the issues of the ***Nintendo Power magazine***, the American magazine dedicated to Nintendo video games. The first issue was published in 1988 and the last one in December 2012.

At the feet of Aech there is a pack of **Lay's chips** and one named ***Ruffles*** both brands are of the historic American producer Frito-Lay. Next to the chips with the yellow package is the **VHS** of the movie by Tim Burton ***Beetlejuice***. On the footrest there are three cans, **Coca Cola**, **Pepsi** and **Tab**, a dietetic beverage produced by the Coca-Cola Company in 1963. In the original language version of Back to the Future, when Marty enters the bar (1955) and the barman asks him to order, he first asks for a Tab. For the Italian market dubbed with "Fanta".

Some of these cans are found around the room. In front of the open box you can see another **VHS** from the movie ***Labyrinth***.

On the right, next to the sofa on which Aech is sitting, there is a bedside table with a lamp, this illuminates the statue of the **golden idol** that is present in the movie ***The Raiders of the Lost Ark***, a 1981 movie directed by Steven Spielberg . Resting on the bedside table is the **Thundercats** toy **sword**, named ***Sword of Omens***.

The wooden pillar illuminated by pink lights is filled with stickers representing the **invaders** of the *Space Invaders* videogame. Hanging on this pillar there are three **prints**. The one below is the **Donkey Kong** flyer developed by Nintendo in 1981, in this game the character of Mario appears for the first time. At the center there is the press of the **Galaga** videogame, in this case it is not the flyer but the full frame sticker that was attached to the side of the cabinet, finally the topmost one is the **Pole Position** flyer. At the base of the column is the **Hover Board** by Marty McFly admired in *Back to the Future Part II* (you will see better in a later shot). At the back of the room is the TV corner of Aech. Above the table there are two **Intellivision Consoles** marketed by Mattel in 1979. Leaning on the sofa is a **Kermit puppet**. On the opposite side of Kermit, still on that table, there is the *Speak & Spell* **electronic game**. At the feet of Kermit the frog is a box of a **Hot Wheels track**, it is the *Electric Racing Formula World Tour*, a version that contains a **Ferrari** and a **McLaren** of F1 with the ability to mount and simulate six different existing circuits: Italy, France, Australia, Germany, Brazil, and United Kingdom.

In front of the mirror, Parzival changes different **clothes**: he wears a **purple coat**, identical to that worn by *Prince* both in the movie and on the cover of the 1984 Purple Rain album. The movie is directed by Albert Magnoli. The **red suit** is like the one worn by *Michael Jackson* in the 1982 Thriller videoclip, directed by John Landis. Then it goes to the punk version, in the back of the **jacket** you can distinguish the **letters DK** of the musical group **Dead Kennedys**, who in his original training worked together from 1978 to 1986. Following, Parzival dresses as **Nick**

Rhodes member of the band *Duran Duran*. Also this group, very popular in the 80s, was formed in 1978. In the end he chooses the dress of the protagonist of the movie **The Adventures of Buckaroo Banzai Across the 8th Dimension** directed by WD Richter (1984).

To the left of the mirror where Parzival in changing, we can see the **poster** of *Goldie Wilson* asking to be re-elected as mayor of Hill Valley, the town of the **movie Back to the Future**. Under the image of Goldie Wilson there is the **poster** of the fantasy movie *The Beastmaster*, in 1982 directed by Don Coscarelli. At the bottom, however, there is a basket with some **album**. The first visible is *Tougher Than Leather* (1988) made by *Run DMC*, this is their fourth album.

On the right of the mirror, at the top there is the "political" **poster** depicting the actor **Wil Wheaton** who is present in the book as vice president of the OASIS, here he appears only in a poster created for the occasion.

Below it is the **poster** of the movie *Mad Max*. Down on the ground there are piles of **magazines** and **comics**. You can still see the magazine *A.N.A.L.O.G.* and on the top of the lower stack is the *DC Comics Swamp Thing* comic number 43, dated December 1985 and written by the genius of Alan Moore. The number is titled "Windfall" and is a special issue because it celebrates 50 years of DC Comics, the story won two Eagle Awards in 1984. On the stack next to the rocking chair you see the historic issue 1 of the **magazine *Nintendo Power*** dated 1988 , another issue can be seen in front of the armchair. Continuing on the right there are: the **poster** of the movie *War Games* (1983) directed by John Badham, the **poster *Big Trouble in Little***

China, above is the **poster** of the actor *Tom Selleck*, next there is a **small poster** of the movie *Labyrinth* (1986) directed by Jim Henson. In the corner bar, Aech has hung on the wall the **electronic date** of the Delorean DMC 12 Back to the Future, this has set the three dates visible in the first demonstration of the journey in time by Doc in Back to the Future. On the bar counter there is a box of **cereals** produced by *Kellogg*, or the *Captain Crunch*, from which a famous Hacker was inspired. In the background stands the The **Peltzer Peeler Juicer**, the juicer invented in the movie Gremlins, next to it is the character of **Cookie Monster** in its toy version (2010) produced in the Cookie Monster's Letter Lunch set by Play-Doh (Hasbro). It is one of the characters of the educational television show for children *Sesame Street* became famous for the participation of the Muppet puppets. The Italian version was called Apriti Sesamo and aired from 1971 to 1978. Behind them is the **poster** depicting the actress *Molly Ringwald*, a very popular actress in the 80s teen movies, protagonist of movies like Breakfast Club, Sixteen Candles and Pretty in Pinl (1986). On the ceiling there are some album hanging, among these we can notice a **mask** related to the robotic character of *Astro Boy*. When Parzival dresses up with Punk on his right at the top next to Goldie Wilson's poster, there's the poster of the 1981 movie Mad Max 2 by George Miller. Below it is the Legend of Zelda poster: A Link to the Past.

The moment Parzival is dressed by one of Duran Duran and Aech is standing behind him he sees a **toy spaceship** at his head, is the model of the *Thunderfight*, a spaceship protagonist of the science-fiction television serial **Buck**

Rogers in the 25th Century. Behind Aech, we can see on the wall to his right a **poster** of *The Raiders of the Lost Ark* and under the poster of *The Fly*, a 1986 movie directed by David Cronenberg. While at the top right, compared to the head of Aech, we see the **poster** banner of the videogame *Space Duel* genre shot'em sequel of Asteroids made in 1982 by Atari and on the opposite side is the **poster banner** of the video game *Missile Command*.

The night at the Distracted Globe

Many **spaceships** are lined up to enter the Distracted Globe. In the foreground appears the Serenity used in the television series *Firefly* in 2002 directed by Joss Whedon and in the movie of the same name.

Among the **spaceships** the mythical *X-Wing* used by the Star Wars rebels and an *Imperial Shuttle* used by the Empire, also in the saga of George Lucas, makes its appearance. The imperial means of Star Wars is accompanied on the left and right by the *Viper* of Battlestar Galactica, behind the left Viper there is a *T-Fighter* used by Imperial soldiers in Star Wars.

Afterwards, Wade is framed while walking on Tapirulan. The image starts from the bottom showing us to his left a *Game Gear*, is a **portable console** produced by SEGA between 1991 and 1997, in front of it a **wrapper** of the *Twix* chocolate snack. On the other side you can glimpse an envelope of *M & M's* chocolate confetti, famous all over the world.

We finally enter the famous Distracted Globe. At the entrance, we can hear the *Blue Monday* **song** of the **New Order** (1988). While Parzival adjusts his tie for a moment to his right we can see the profile of **Duke Nukem**. Parzival immediately crosses the villain of the DC Comics **Deathstroke** universe which passes to his left. Then look at the top floating characters, among them there is **Gandalf the gray** from the trilogy of The Lord of the Rings and of Lo Hobbit both directed by Peter Jackson and taken from the fantasy stories of J.R.R. Tolkien.

When the shot returns to Parzival, in the background, **El Dragon** is seen as a character in the **Battleborn** videogame. At the Distracted Globe, all robotic baristas wear **hats** from **Devo's "Whip It" music video**. The group name is printed on the bartenders' chest.

When Art3mis and Parzival meet in front of the bar of the restaurant we can distinguish a skeleton (the place is full) and in the background **Blanka** from **Street Fighter** and **Chun-Li** from **Street Fighter II**, you will also see dancing in a later scene. On the left is **Shepard**'s character, the protagonist of BioWare's videogame **Mass Effect** in 2007. Before the shot passes on the feet of I-R0k you can see **Lara Croft** approaching the counter. While I-R0k is about to enter the private room, it is possible to see **Wonder Woman** among the characters on the background to his left.

When I-R0k takes a seat in the disco sofas, we can well distinguish the DC Comics character **Harley Quinn**. Around Art3mis and Parzival, in addition to the aforementioned **Blanka** and **Chun Li**, there is **Zitz**, a character from **Battletoads**, who talks with **Miko** about the **Battleborn** videogame. Behind them is **Ambra** from the video game **Battleborn**. The track scenes also reveal **Sub Zero** by **Mortal Kombat** and **Ryu** by **Street Fighter**.

The dance that begins Parzival is taken from the movie **Saturday Night Fever** (1977) by John Badham, in the background there is the homonym **song** by Bee Gees, also from 1977. Wade choose the song whose album is displayed on the screen of his viewer. Even the dance floor that is formed is taken from that movie with John Travolta.

Art3mis, to dance the Saturday Night Fever song by Bee

Gees, transforms her skirt into a pair of flamboyant bell-bottoms from the '70s.

As soon as they start to dance, a short scene shows **Tracer**, from the video game *Overwatch*, who turns to look at the two dancers. Same as **Kitana** from the video game *Mortal Kombat* and an avatar that looks a lot like **Blastoise**, the famous character of *Pokemon*, video game created by Nintendo. Even the **Joker**, well-known comic book character DC Comics turns around to watch the scene. Here it is presented in the version seen in the comic *Batman: Killing Joke*, written by Alan Moore and designed by Brian Bolland. Along with him is **Harley Quinn** in the video game version *Batman: Arkham Knight*.

When the agents of the IOI burst, Art3mis reveals his weapon by holding the **M41A impulse shotgun**, the same one used by the character of Sigourney Weaver in *Aliens*, a sci-fi movie directed by James Cameron in 1986. Parzival holds, in his right hand, the **Colonial Warrior Blaster** used in the original *Battlestar Galactica* series from the 70s. After it is hit, Parzival uses a **Lazer Tag**. This is a toy gun produced by Worlds of Wonder in 1986. After the two are hit by I-R0k, Art3mis extracts a **Lawgiver** in his right hand, which is the gun that uses Sylvester Stallone in the role *of Judge Dreed* in the movie Judge Dreed (1995), directed by Danny Cannon. When the Zemeckis cube is used, the re-arranged motif composed by Alan Silvestri for the movie **Back to the Future** can be heard.

Outside of OASIS

When Wade comes out of OASIS and finds himself in the van behind him there is a solved maze. The box, to which the labyrinth hangs, contains a **Game Boy Advance**, a Nintendo 32 BIT handheld console from 2001. Next to it is a Nintendo Game Boy.

After the dance, and after the curtain between Sorrento and F'Nale Zandor, there is an overview of the piles while Wade returns to his van. In one of the walls there is a visible **graffiti**, it is a reproduction of the famous *Madballs*, this is blue. At the top right of the Madball there is a small drawing depicting **Mike Wazowski** star of the animated movie *Pixar Monsters & Co.* (Monster Inc.) (2001) directed by Pete Docter.

At the moment when Wade touches the **prism** to accept the invitation of Sorrento we can see a play of light that is a reference to the cover of the album *The Dark Side of the Moon* by Pink Floyd (1973).

Parzival meets Sorrento

In the first monologue of Sorrento this makes several references to pop culture of the '80s: nomination of the video game **Defender**, the **Millennium Falcon**, the spaceship of Han Solo in the Star Wars saga. He quotes director **John Hughes**. the movie **Breakfast Club** and his school, the **High School in Shermer**. Name the movie

Ferris Bueller's Day Off. Parzival tries to deceive him, but his collaborators point out that 1982 is not directed by John Hughes but *Amy Heckerling*, written by Cameron Crowe. And that the **University of Faber** is that of the 1978 movie by John Landis **Animal House**. Among the other elements of popular culture mentioned are the **Tab** drink, the video game **Robotron**, made by Williams Electronics in 1982, it is a fixed screen shooter. The full name of the game is Robotron: 2084. **Duran Duran** is named for music. While Sorrento speaks, in the background you can see bulletin boards with various objects, one of which contains, hanging on the top left, the gun used by **Captain Malcolm Reynolds** in the TV series *Firefly*.

Sorrento also tells Wade to know where he lives, that is, in the **56K** unit of the stacks in Columbus. 56K is the abbreviation of 56kbit / s, which is the maximum transmission speed that was given by analogue modems put on the market in 1995.

To suggest the words to Sorrento are the Members of oology, and during this comparison in their sector C7 the monitor on the right shows a scene of the movie Fast Times at Ridgemont High (1982) directed by Amy Heckerling, the monitor on the left instead shows a short scene from **Breakfast Club**. When the editing takes us back to the oology room, on the right monitor, the cover of the Duran Duran **Arena** disc (1984) appears. This is replaced, a few moments later, by the **Rio** album cover, always Duran Duran (1982).

In the rebels' den

Wade's kidnapper wears a **T-shirt** from the *Devo* band and on the left arm he **tattooed** a typical screen of the *Space Invaders videogame*. While Samantha, in the real world, wears a **T-shirt** that has the design of the album cover *Unkown Pleasure*, the first of the Joy Divisions dated 1979.

The phrase that pronounces Samantha **"welcome in the rebellion"** is a quote from the sentence pronounced by Jyn Erso in *Rogue One: A Star Wars Story*, a spin-off movie from the original saga, directed by Gareth Edwards in 2016. In the wall of the lair, where drawn the face of the Aztec, there is the writing **"Level Up"**, a significant word in the world of video games that is identified with the increase in player level.

In the opposite wall, the graffiti represents a blue *Madball* with red pupil and white bandages.

On the visor of Samantha there is a **sticker** with the logo of *Batman* by Tim Burton, and one that represents the cherries of *Pac-Man*. In the game, in the middle of the screen appears for a little bit of the fruit that must be eaten to accumulate points.

The movie that Halliday has seen

When Parzival asks the curator to show him the movies seen by Halliday in November 2025 from the ceiling, before and after they make the decision to enter Shining, they drop like videotapes. During this scene we recognized the **covers** of: *The Fly* (1986) by David Cronenberg (also nominated by Art3mis), ***Say Anything... (1989)*** directed by Cameron Crowe (also nominated by Art3mis), ***Biloxi Blues*** from 1984 directed by Mike Nichols, ***War Games*** by John Badham from 1983, ***Lost Boys*** by Joel Schumacher from 1987, ***Blade Runner*** by Ridley Scott from 1982, ***The Shining*** by Stanley Kubrick, ***Alien*** (1979) by Ridley Scott, Risky Business (1983) movie written and directed by Paul Brickman, ***ET The extraterrestrial*** by Steven Spielberg (1982), Tim Burton's 1989 ***Batman***, Stanley Kubrick's ***Full Metal Jacket*** 1987, ***Back to the Future - Part II*** (1989) directed by Robert Zemeckis, **Scarface** (1983) directed by Brian De Palma, ***Superman II*** (1980) by Richard Lester, and always by the same director Superman III (1983), ***Firestarter*** (1984) directed by Mark L. Lester, ***Breakfast Club*** (1985) directed by John Hughes, **Airplane** (1980) directed by the trio Zucker, Ambrahams, Zucker, ***Lethal Weapon*** 2 (1989) by Richard Donner, ***Beverly Hills Cop*** (1984) by Martin Best, ***Innerspace*** (1987) directed by Joe Dante and produced by Steven Spielberg, ***Vision Quest*** (1985) directed by Harold Becker, Joe Dante's ***The Burbs*** by 1989.

When Parzival chooses Shining, in the real world, both

Wade and Samantha are seen wearing their respective viewers. Both but in different places have the **Street Fighter sticker**.

92

The Overlook

The scene begins with the **Shining musical theme** composed by Wendy Carlos and Rachel Elking.

It is immediately clear to the eye that the cinema that projects The Shining is called The Overlook, which is the same name as the Hotel of which Jack Torrance becomes custodian in Kubrick's movie.

To the left of the entrance there are **two posters**, the farther away is **_Wargames_** and next to that of **_Flash Gordon_**, a 1980 movie directed by Mike Hodges. To the right of the entrance there are two more **posters**, the rightmost is that of the movie **_Excalibur_**, a 1981 fantasy movie directed by John Boorman, next to it is the **_Star Wars Episode VI - Return of the Jedi_** (1983) movie that concludes the original saga of George Lucas.

The whole sequence to get the second key is set in Kubrick's movie. The text of the typewriter, the same as the movie in the American language, takes the form of the key. Aech pulls the **tennis ball against the elevator door**, taking up the gesture made by Jack Nicholson when he throws it against the wall in the movie.

The **twins** appear who, after talking with Aech, enter the elevator, but in the movie we find them simply in the corridor.

The **blood flood** scene shown in the first The Shining trailer in 1980 was also recreated.

While Aech is carried by the current of blood he tries to stop putting his hands on the wall. Here we can see the famous

photo of 1921 with Halliday in place of Jack Torrance and next to him Kira.

Room 237 is the same as the movie, Aech is found falling into the same trap made to Jack Torrance. The same Aech, is attacked by an **axe that breaks through the door**. In Kubrick's movie, Jack's character breaks through the bathroom door where his wife Wendy and her son Danny have taken refuge.

When Aech finds himself in the **snowy labyrinth**, a low angle view shows the limping feet of Jack Torrance chasing Aech. After the scene of the maze you enter the hotel again and the group of three runs, because the time available is expiring. Behind them is **Danny's tricycle**.

In the ballroom, Art3mis recognizes that the moment is similar to a level of the Logic Obscure Productions video game **Mayhem Mansion**.

When you return to the headquarters of the IOI, it is noted in Sorrento the update of the scoreboard related to the race score to the public. On this occasion, when the camera focuses on the tablet, we can see in the area of the Community Feed, at the bottom left, some nicknames that flow. These include **Berris Fueller** and **Copo Rob**: the first is a reference to the protagonist of the movie *Ferris Bueller's Day Off*, Ferris Bueller, replacing, in the nickname, the initial letter of the name with that of the surname and vice versa you get the name of the character played by Matthew Broderick. The second is an acronym, Copo Rob easily becomes *Robocop*, the title of the movie of the same name.

In the rebels' den: the notebook

The notebook of Samantha's notes should be carefully observed. In the sheet on the left there is the inscription **"I am Sanchez Villalobos Ramirez"** which is the character played by Sean Connery in the movie *Highlander*, in 1986 directed by Russell Mulcahy. The Highlander title is written further down. It refers to the motion of **Kaneda** in Akira and *The Princess Diaries*, a romantic comedy (2001) directed by Garry Marshall and based on the 2000 novel of the same name. **Sixteen Candles** a teenage comedy movie written and directed by John Hughes in 1984.

In the right-hand sheet within the first sentence there are the words **"number"** and **"magic"** the last word circled, it is connected to **"*School House Rock*"** also circled. School House Rock is an American animated television series broadcast from 1973 to 2009. The magic number as written several times in the sheet is **3**. Under the hoop of the word School House Rock it says: **Indiana Jones** and under **Gremlins**, follows **Dark Crystal**. Next to it is **Neverending Story**, fantastic movie (1984), directed by Wolfgang Petersen. In another shot of the right page we can see the writings referring to **Indiana Jones and the Temple of Doom** (1984) directed by Steven Spielberg, **Krull** (1983) directed by Peter Yates, **Splash** (1984) directed by Ron Howard. In addition there is the inscription **"Helm's Deep"** a reference to the *Lord of the Rings* written by JRR Tolkien and published in 1954. Helm's Deep is the Fosso di Helm where one of the great battles of the history of the book is held. also the second movie in the Peter Jackson trilogy. Follow **The Hitchhiker's Guide to the Galaxy**. Under it we read **"42"**, an **"important"** number in the *Galactic Guide for hitchhikers*. The fundamental number for the solution of the last quest will be together with the **"3"**.

Aech's Van

Before entering the van you can see a **graffiti** with orange outline that reproduces the heroine of the comics DC Comics **Raven**, created by Marv Wolfman and George Pérez in 1980.

The **demonic face** on the back door of the van is taken from the adventure of Dungeon & Dragons *Tomb of Horror*, written by Gary Gygax in 1975.

When Sho and Daito are together with their backs there is the **sticker** of Tim Burton's 1989 *Batman logo*. While, on the left side of Daito there is a **sticker** of the *Cabbage Patch Kids*. These dolls were designed by Debbie Morehead and Xavier Roberts in 1978.

Helen's clothing

On Helen **T-shirt** is the design of the cover of the *album 2112* of the *Rush* (1976).

On the left side the jacket has a **patch** that represents the *Wonder Woman logo* of the '70s. At the top there is the **patch** with the writing *DK*: initials of the band Dead Kennedys, founded in 1978. There is also the heroine DC Comics *Supergirl logo*. On the left shoulder there is the **patch** with the legendary lips that represent the cult movie (1975), directed by Jim Sharman, *The Rocky Horror Picture Show*. There is also a **red pin** whose white writing is "*Supergirl*".

On the right side there is the same *Wonder Woman logo* of the 70s and also the **DK** patch. There is the **pin** of the *Simon* game and the one representing a 20-sided die (*D20*). There is a large **patch** of *Wonder Woman* with her arms crossed in the version designed by George Perez.

There are three **patches** dedicated to *Thundercats*: *Cheetara*, **Lion-O** and *Wilykit*.

The Last Key

The last clue reads "If you know the definitive answer divide it by the magic number and what you need, you want and you will find in the tragic fort."

The number to be divided by **42** in reference to the work **The Hitchhiker's Guide to the Galaxy**, 42 has to be divided by 3, the magic number of the TV series **School House of Rock**. The result is 14 which is the sector in which the third key is located. The planet of the last challenge resembles the volcanic planet **Mustafar**, a key location in episode III of the Star Wars saga.

The soldiers of the IOI are playing with the **Atari VCS 2600 console**. When they are observed by the avatar of Sorrento, the first **game** we see is *Gravitar* (1983). Then it is played **Centipede** (1982) and then **Adventure** (1979).

Retur in oology room

When the movie takes us to the oology room, the following cartridges are thrown on the table: **Donkey Kong** (1983), **Laserblast** (1981), **Joust** (1983), **Defender** (1982). One of the components of the oology, the boy with the beard, throws on the table the *Joust* videogame **box**.

On the table we can see the book **The Hitchhiker's Guide to the Galaxy by** Douglas Adams and above it there is the book **Life, the universe and everything** always the same author, this is the third book of the saga. Also two

chocolate snacks recognizable in *Snickers* and *Twix*.

Behind the girl with long red hair there is a blackboard. This shows some places that could be in the area of 14. **Hogwarts Castle**, it is the castle home to the school of magic and witchcraft in the fantasy world Harry Potter created by the English writer J. K. Rowling. The series of seven books was published between 1997 and 2007. It follows a movie franchise, spin-offs and a play. The **Hornburgs** (it was the ancient name used by the men of Gondor) referring to the Lord of the Rings. **Hyrule Castle** is a location in the *Nintendo Legends of Zelda* series of video games. **Isengard**, which is the home of Saruman in The Lord of the Rings, **Minas Morgul** is the dead city of the Nazgul in The Lord of the Rings. **Miraz's Castle** which is the castle of Prince Caspian, which is part of the saga of the *Chronicles of Narnia*, created by C.S. Lewis from whom movies have also been made. **The Castle of Otranto** is a novel by Horace Walpole of 1764, considered the first Gothic novel. **Princess Peach** Castle which is the castle where Princess Peach lives, a character from the *Nintendo saga world*.

I-R0k activate the Osuvox globe

The spell that pronounces I-R0k is exactly the same spell used by **Merlin** to turn Uther into the face of his enemy in the movie ***Excalibur,*** directed by John Boorman in 1981. The spell is called "Charm of Making" and reads: "Ahnahl nathrakh, uhr vahss bethud, dochthiel tienveigh. "Translated:" It is the breath of the serpent, enchantment of death and life, your omen of doing. "

Parzival and Daito meet Sorrento

Wade and Daito (dressed in black) hold Nolan hostage in a virtual reality within OASIS. Another virtual reality, this is a clear reference to the movie **Inception** (2010) by Christopher Nolan. Once again, Parzival removes the Wade mask as in a **Mission Impossible** movie.
After a few minutes Daito remains alone with Sorrento, in his eyes the **yellow** of the pupils recalls that of the replicants of ***Blade Runner.***

Samantha in the Sorrento office

When Samantha is seated at the Sorrento station, she scrolls through the database of the head of the IOI. Among them he mentions **"all Nancy Drew's novels"**. Nancy Drew is the female protagonist of a series of children's crime novels published in the United States of America since the 1930s, in Italy they arrived in the 60s. Kegel exercises that are used to develop the muscles of the pelvic area, often prescribed to solve incontinence problems. This is evidently a mockery of the character of Sorrento.

The Final Battle

When Parzival calls all the citizens of OASIS to collect, the object that takes him on video is clearly a billiard **ball number 8**. This cam is very similar to an *8-ball*, a toy produced until the 80s that was able to "predict the future". To support the protagonist of the movie is **The Iron Giant**, which we will see for the rest of the movie. This is activated by Helen even if incomplete.

When Wade is framed, on this new viewer we can see two different colored **stickers** of a *20-sided die*. On the other side, it has a **sticker** produced by *Santa Cruz Screaming Hand*, a company founded in 1973. On the side, at the left ear level, there is the **sticker** with the *The Greatest American Hero logo*. Daito instead has on the collar of the visor a **sticker** with the logo of **Mortal Kombat** and one with that of **Batman**.

During the speech, Parzival names **Gygax'**s gold mines as a place. Gygax is the surname of *Gary Gygax* who together with Dave Arneson created the role-playing game Dungeon & Dragons in 1974. On OASIS listening to the call of Parzival there is a large group of **characters** already seen as the *Wolf Man, Darryl "DMC" McDaniels, Arkham Knight, Cappy, Catwoman, Aquaman*.

When Sorrento sees the army of the citizens of OASIS arriving he feels discouraged and I-R0k thinks well to console it by quoting Frank Capra's movie *It's a Wonderful Life* (1946), the phrase he uses is "No man is a failure if he has some friends" .

From this moment on, the movie has an alternate montage between the final battle outside and inside the fortress and between reality and OASIS. You will find below the topics divided by macro areas.

Again in the Oology room

Whenever a member of the IOI fails in front of the **Atari VCS 2600 console**, the members of oology mark the situation in their notes. The following games are on the board in which the key may be hidden:

Centipede developed by Atari in 1981 (played) - porting for Atari VCS 2600 in 1982.

Joust developed by Williams Electronics in 1982 - porting for Atari VCS 2600 in 1983.

Adventure developed by Atari in 1980 (played)

Pac-Man developed by Namco in 1980 - porting for Atari VCS 2600 in 1982.

Bridge developed by Activision in 1981.

Swordquest, in this case the blackboard does not indicate which chapter of the saga has been played. The saga is composed of the following titles: **Swordquest: Earthworld** (1982), Swordquest: Fireworld (1983), **Swordquest: Waterworld** (1984) (played).

Motocross developed by Atari (1983).

Defender developed by Williams Electronics in 1981 - porting for Atari VCS 2600 in 1982.

Dice Puzzle developed by Panda Computer Games in 1983.

Racquetball developed by Apollo in 1981.

Dragon Treasure developed by Zellers in 1982.

Winter Games developed by Epyx in 1987.

Dumbo's Flying Circus developed by Atari in 1983.

E. T. The Extra-Terrestrial developed by Atari in 1982 (played).

Fantastic Voyage developed by Sirius Software in 1982.

Battlezone developed by Atari in 1980 - porting for Atari VCS 2600 in 1983.

Eggo mania developed by US games 1982.

Fast Eddie developed by Sirius Software in 1982.

Firefly developed by Mythicon in 1983.

Exocet developed by Panda Computer Games in 1983.

Espial developed by Tigervision in 1984 (played), is one of the 10 rarest games of the Atari VCS 2600.

Fathom developed by Imagic in 1983.

Fast Food developed by Telesys in 1982 (played).

Wall ball developed by Avalon Hill in 1983.

Confrontation developed by Answer Software in 1983.

Artillery Duel developed by Xonox in 1983.

Pitfall developed by Activision in 1982.

Flash Gordon developed by Sirius Software in 1983.

Fire Fighters developed by Imagic in 1982.

Buck Rogers: Planet of Zoom developed by SEGA in 1983.

Bugs developed by Data Age in 1982.

Bashers Bash developed by Spectra Vision in 1983.

Bump 'n' Jump developed by Data East in 1982 - porting for Atari VCS 2600 in 1983.

Burger Time developed by Data East in 1982 - porting for

Atari VCS 2600 in 1982.

Carnival developed by SEGA in 1980 - porting for Atari VCS 2600 in 1982.

Challenge of nexar developed by Sirius Software in 1982.

China Syndrome developed by Spectra Vision in 1983.

Chopper Command developed by Activision in 1982.

Cosmic Commuter developed by Activision in 1984.

Cosmic Crips developed by Telesis in 1982.

Crackpots developed by Activision in 1983.

Cakewalk developed by CommaVid in 1983.

Chase the chuck wagon developed by Tmq Software in 1983.

Deadly Discs developed by Telegames in 1983.

Deadly Dark, but in reality the game would be Deadly **Duck**. developed by Sirius Software in 1982. We believe that it is a mistake of transcription on the blackboard since there is no game with the name they reported for the Atari VCS 2006 console.

Deathtrap developed by Avalon Hill in 1983.

Demon Attack developed by Imagic in 1982.

Dolphin developed by Activision in 1983.

Bacherolette Party developed by Mystique in 1982.

Beat Em and Eat Em developed by Mystique in 1982.

Bermuda Triangle developed by Data Age in 1982.

Acid Drop developed by Dennis Kiss in 1992, this is the last game created for the Atari VCS 2006 console.

Actionauts developed by Rob Fulop in 2008, the curiosity is that the video game project is ready since 1984 but it was never realized before 2008.

Near one of the windows there is a cart with movie posters resting, these are the original posters of the movie **Weird Science**, directed in 1985 by John Hughes.

Osuvox active

Among the avatars running towards Parzival and passing by are:

Three **Battletoad, Zitz, Rash,** and **Pimple,** from the 1991 video game of the same name for SNES (Nintendo). On their left is **Tokka,** character of the second animated series of **Teenage Mutant Ninja Turtle.** This character is also seen in the second movie (1991) Tartarughe Ninja II - The secret of Ooze. Behind them on the right is **El Dragon,** the character of the video game **Battleborn.** We also see one of the **flying ostriches** of the videogame **Joust.**

There is the **StarCraft Marine** from the 1998 **StarCraft** videogame. Ray Harryhausen's **Cyclops** seen in **The 7th Sinbad Journey** (1958). There are also the usual skeletons with helmets and swords ready for battle.

In addition to **Halo**'s **Master Chief** we also see a Grunt (Unggony) always taken from the Halo video game.

Osuvox disabled

In the foreground there is **Tracer,** next to the left is **Chun-Li.** Between Chun-Li and Tracer there is **FemShepard,** Jane protagonist of **Mass Effect 3** made by BioWare in 2007 and you can also see **Amber** character of the video game **Battleborn** behind them with the stick in hand. To the right of Tracer is **Turner** the anthropomorphic rabbit, from the video game **Lugaru** created by Wolfire Games in 2005 for computers.

Behind Turner is **Lara Croft**, and behind her is **Rayne** starring in the series of ***BloodRayne*** video games made by Terminal Reality in 2002.

Framed on the right is a battalion of skeletons.

A **Na'avi** can be glimpsed behind Lara Croft. Na'avi are characters from James Cameron's 2008 movie ***Avatar.*** Between Tracer and Lara Croft is **Sergeant Cassandra Carlton Cage** of the special forces of Earthrealm, also known as Cassie. Protagonist of ***Mortal Kombat X*** created by NetherRealm Studios in 2015; is the daughter of two important protagonists of the game saga Johnny Cage and Sonya Blade. To the right of Lara Croft is **Catwoman** from the DC Comics universe. Ready for battle there is a **squadron of Masterchief** from the video game ***Halo***, along with them on the left side there is Unggoy and on the right side there is a **Sanghelli Elite Ultra** both from the ***Halo*** videogame universe. Behind them, and for a very short frame and not a full figure, there's Toby from **Battleborn**.

In the new sequence there are the avatar of **Spawn**, character of the homonym comic book created by Todd McFarlane in 1992.

To the right of Spawn there is **Batgirl**, behind her there is **Flash**, comic book character DC Comics, version taken from the video game ***Injustice 2*** developed by NetherRealm Studios in 2017.

To the right of Flash, there is **Aquaman**, you notice his trident. Aquaman was created by Mort Weisinger and Paul Norris in 1941. To the right of Aquaman is **Cyborg**, another DC Comics character.

To the left of Spawn is **He-Man**, the protagonist of the action figure series called *Masters of the Universe* (1981), which later became an animated series entitled He-Man and the Masters of the Universe. Then also a movie in 1987 directed by Gary Goddard titled The Dominators of the Universe.

There is **Joker** and **Robocop** is visible to his left. In front of everyone there is the bad **Gremlin** "Stripe" taken from the homonym movie by Joe Dante (1984).

Parzival raises a **Sharp GF-7600 Radio Cassette Boombox** (1980). The action he performs is identical to that of Lloyd Dobler (John Cusack), or the protagonist of *Say anything...* .

We hear the **Twisted Sister - *We're Not Gonna Take* It song** from 1984.

Arriving from behind are **Sagat**, a character from the *Street Fighter* videogame and **Deadshot** villain from the comics universe DC Comics.

Frontal Clash

When the army of Parzival faces that of the IOI, on the first panoramic shot, we can see on the left **two lions** of the animated series ***Voltron: Defend of the Universe*** that run in unison. The series is distributed in America by World Events Production in 1983. The latter assembled two different series made by Toei Animation: Golion and Armored Fleet Dairugger XV making it look like a unique series.

Among the characters in action there is **Honda** of the video game ***Street Fighter*** that goes against the enemy lines. There is a very fast **Sonic the Hedgedog** between the legs of many characters.

Immediately after **Chun Li** performed with a high kick. While Art3mis does a somersault in the air, you see on his left the character of **Unggoy** from the universe of ***Halo***.

While Art3mis tries to reunite with Parzival, passes next to a soldier of the IOI who is brutally attacked by **four Gremlins**, one of these has the ***hat of Santa Claus*** and **another the 3D glasses** in classic red and blue. Later we see the **Wolfman** again.

Parzival's DeLorean enters the scene

To take down the armored vehicle, on which Art3mis has risen, Parzival uses an **SPNKr rocket launcher**, the iconic weapon of the ***Halo*** videogame.

On board the DeLorean Art3mis and Parzival continue to shoot with more weapons and Parzival uses the **shotgun Sawn-off**, with the addition of sight, which holds the protagonist of the movie *Mad Max*. When the ammunitions end, the girl passes the **Tesla Cannon - Anti-personnel order cannon** (Anti-Personnel Ordnance Cannon) in the *Overwatch* videogame.

While Parzival will get the **Railgun**, which the gamers have seen in *Duke Nuken Forever* (2011). Let's see in action the giant **Cyclops** of Ray Harryhousen and later Helen passes the doll **Chucky**, protagonist of the homonymous horror movie saga, to Parzival that throws it against the members of the IOI. Among the fighters there are the four **Ninja Turtles**, here in their latest movie version. **Halo's military squadron** battles with a group of warrior skeletons. In this final battle we meet again a scorpion taken from the **Ultrabots** videogame.

Sorrento uses Mechagodzilla

Mecha Godzilla is a villain of the *Godzilla* movie franchise. Mecha Godzilla made his first appearance in the 14th movie of the Godzilla saga entitled Godzilla against the robots (Gojira tai Mekagojira), (1974) directed by Jun Fukuda.

One can hear the "Godzilla March", the **musical theme** of *Godzilla* by Akira Ifukube (1954).

Mechagodzilla is defeated by Art3mis thanks to an explosive **Madballs** after fighting against **Gundam RX-78**, robot of the animated series (1979) created by Yoshiyuki Tomino. The Gundam is released by the spaceship **Serenity** star of Joss Whedon's 2002 television series Firefly. This version of Gundam has two particularities compared to that of the animated series.

On the left shoulder, there is in fact printed the initials **WB** in reference to the producer of the movie Ready Player One, *Warner Bros*. On the right shoulder is the abbreviation **EFSP** which stands for *Earth Federation Space Force*. It is a terrestrial military apparatus present in the Gundam saga.

Arrival at the Castle

When our heroes have crossed the bridge formed by the body of the **Iron Giant**, Art3mis is looking for a weapon to use from his menu. Among these is **the Lazer Tag**, the **Sniper Rifle Invader** model created by Hyperion in the video game **Bordelands 2**; it is a first person shooter action RPG, sequel to the 2009 video game Borderlands was released in 2012 by Gearbox Software. However, Art3mis can not select any of the two weapons, so he takes the **Lancer Rifle Chainsaw**. This assault rifle with a chainsaw is a weapon *of Gears of War*, made by Epic Games in 2008.When the Iron Giant falls into the lava, he raises his thumb in a sign of **"everything is OK"** like in the movie *Terminator 2 - The Day of Judgment* (1991) by James Cameron when the gesture is the T-800 played by Arnold Schwarzenegger. Sho, at this point, uses the weapon **Glaive** which is a hooked star capable of cutting the arm of I-R0k. This weapon is used by the protagonist of Peter Yates's 1983 movie *Krull*.

The weapon with which Parzival "kills" Art3mis is the **Standard Colonial Blaster,** the protagonist of the television series *Battlestar Galattica*.

During the fight between Sorrento and Wade, the latter unleashes a **"hadouken"** on Sorrento. Ryu's special move in the Street Fighter video game.

Meanwhile, in real life, while Aech drives the van hoping to escape from the pursuers he makes a joke and names the video game **Mario Kart**. This is a video game made by

Nintendo in 1992 whose full name is Super Mario Kart.

The explosion of the Catalyst and I-R0k treasure

The treasure of I-R0k includes: a yellow rubber duck, these toy ducks used in the bathtubs were made famous by Jim Henson in the 70s. There is a sample of Nike Powerlace shoe used by Marty McFly in Back to the Future Part II, two videocassettes with different covers by Scarface, movie (1983) with Al Pacino directed by Brian De Palma, the shield of Perseus that the protagonist of the movie Clash of Titans, a VHS of the movie Pee-wee's Big Adventure 1985 directed by Tim Burton, there is the basic rules book of Dungeon's & Dragons dated 1977, a comic about Swamp Thing - number 43 of the 1980 published by DC comics.

All the previously mentioned avatars are overwhelmed by the explosion. We distinguish the following characters: skeletons, Attikus and El Dragon characters of the video game Battleborn, Jason Voorhees protagonist of the movie saga Friday 13, Freddy Kruger star of the movie saga Nightmare, Batgirl super heroine of the DC Comics, Ryu protagonist of the video game Street Fighter, and Master Chief of Halo

Oology room after the explosion

After using the extra life the members of oology start to follow the Parzival that play **Adventure** videogame. In the screen of one of them, before the screens go into live streaming mode, you notice that he is playing a game of *Final Lap* **video game** made by Namco in 1987, here in his Japanese version. To the left of the monitor is the **comic book Legionnaries number 9** (1993) published by DC Comics. Behind the screen you can see the **cover** of the *Rush 2112* album. While the two members of oology walk towards the screen to follow the live stand **two DC comics** stand out on the table, lower left *Green Lantern Corps number 224* (May 1988), on the upper part on the right is the *Superman number 376* (October 1982) both published by DC comics. Shortly thereafter on the table there is a **Nintendo Nes 8Bit** followed by a second copy. In the second luminous wall containing a comic table we see an advertising page related to the launch of the **Flash Gordon comic** book for DC Comics. Subsequently, on a cart are placed movie **posters**, the visible one is from the movie *Weird Science*, while on the table there is a console Colecovision.

Last challenge

Before returning to OASIS to discovery that Parzival is still alive, on the left side of the van, on the door, there is a drawing of a **Beholder**, the famous monstrous creature of ***Dungeons & Dragons***.

The viewer that Samantha holds shows three **stickers** dedicated to ***Wonder Woman, the logo*** in the middle, the face on the left and a half-length of the heroine DC Comics on the right.

After Parzival inserts the three keys into what looks like a safe, a window opens up onto a room where Halliday's golden light glows. The style is very similar to the dome of the **Basilica of St. Peter in the Vatican** created by Michelangelo in the mid-1500s.

The throne is formed by the dragons of the video game Mortal Kombat. In the upper right corner of the throne room there is **Raiden** a playable character of the video game, whose first appearance is marked in ***Mortal Kombat I*** (1992). In the lower left corner there is **Scorpion** whose first appearance always happens in ***Mortal Kombat I*** as well as for **Sub-Zero** placed in the lower right corner. In the upper right corner there is **Kitana** whose appearance is in 1993 in ***Mortal Kombat II.***

At the top of the room there is a writing that reads: "*Three hidden keys open three secret gates. Where in the errant will be tested for worthy traits. Those with the skill to survive these straits. Will reach The End where the prize awaits*"

Parzival is about to sign the contract and then stops. The

"**choice**" scene resembles that of Steven Spielberg's Indiana Jones movie and the latest crusade when ***Indiana Jones*** is about to take the wrong Holy Grail by being fooled by the presence of gold.

Sorrento at the Stacks

At one point, Sorrento is stopped by a woman who tells him that she knows what he did to the stacks (referring to the explosions caused). This woman has a **T-shirt** that brings as a design the **cover** of the ***Technique*** album (1989) of the ***New Order***. Sorrento is then surrounded, including a man wearing the **MotörHead** t-shirt with reference to the 1980 ***Ace of spade*** album. Another man wears a t-shirt from the ***Iron Maiden*** group. A man, wearing a headgear, wears a ***Dirty Ghetto Kids* t-shirt** (DGK) an American skateboard company.

Halliday's Room

Halliday wears the **t-shirt** of the *Space Invaders* videogame, the **pins** on the jacket are: the one related to the electronic game *Simon*, the one with the inscription "*I am the keymaster*" in reference to *Ghostbusters*, that of the, *D20* and as fourth there is one that represents the bar of OASIS. The walls of the room are full of Halliday's drawings that prove to be a good designer and an astronomer enthusiast. On the table, near the left wall, a **game** of *Advanced Dungeons & Dragons* is ready, you can see the character cards, game miniatures, pencils and the Master's screen in its first edition (1979). This screen consisted of two modules 2 and 4 sides respectively. Under the small table, placed at the sloping wall, you see the *Connect 4* game by Milton Bradley (MB) edition made in 1984. To the right of the door, above the chest of drawers there is a recorder coils and placed on it the *Firefox F-7* **portable videogame**, realized by Grandstand in 1983. Under the button to cancel OASIS there are some **joysticks/pad** hanging, among these there are *two SEGA Genesis 6 Button Controller Pad* (1993), a *Konix Speedking* and an *Atari 2600 joystick controller.* Still on the floor, there are board games on the floor. We recognize the first on top which is *Thunder Road* published in 1986 by Milton Bradley. This is a car race simulation in a post-apocalyptic future, a bit like Mad Max. Next to it you can see an Anderson *Jacobson A211 Acoustic Coumpler modem*, which allowed the first connections between computers in the '80s.

On the left wall, above a desk, is a 1987 **Macintosh II Apple.**

The Halliday child version wears a *Space Invaders* videogame different in design and color from that of his alter ego. He is playing the *Gorf* **videogame** with a **Colecovision** console marketed in 1982. Beside the console there are various cartridges, not only for Colecovision, but also for Atari and they are: *Pac-Man, Space Invaders, Missile Command, Defender, Pole Position, and Root Beer Tapper* (1984); the game is a port of the homonym coin-op made by Midway. To the left of the Colecovision you can see an **Anderson Jacobson A211 Acoustic Coumpler modem.** To the right of the Colecovision there is a wireless cordless typical of the 80s, near there is a **retrogames emulator** inside a modified box of the *Gameboy Nintendo.* Above it is the **mini arcade** *FL U-Boat* made by Bandai in 1982 and to the right **handheld** *Space Turbo* (1985) made by Tomy, curiously without the cloche.

On the cabinet, in front of the window, there is an **Instant Camera by Kodak,** it is the *Colorburst 100* model also known as EK100 produced in 1978 and made for the U.S.A. and for Canada until 1980. On the cabinet there are several photos taken. In front there is a **View-Master Model G** made in Belgium. It is a stereoscopic vision system first produced by Sawyers, from 1959 to 1977. The View-Master is equipped with a focusing system for particular slides mounted on disks. These disks are present on the trunk that is positioned in front of the cabinet where we saw the Macintosh II. On the other side of the cabinet, in front of the window, there is an **electronic Mattel Synsonic (Type**

Drum Machine) battery sold in 1985. Between the TV stand and the cabinet in front of the window there is a **Gumball Machine**, a dispenser of chewing gum in the shape of a ball. At the foot of the cabinet in front of the window there is a **chessboard** and next to a *Big Trak Milton Bradley* (1979), it is a **programmable vehicle**. Behind it is visible the *Robby The Robot* **toy box** that we see above the table to the right of Halliday child. This version of the toy is an authentic replica in 1/5 scale 16 inches (40.6 cm) tall that speaks while lighting up the front of the mouth. The toy was produced by Masudaya in 1984. On this table there is also a **Lava Lamp**.

To the right of Halliday child there is the **game *Rock 'Em Sock' Em Robots***, it is a ring where two robots, one red and one blue, practice boxing. The first edition of this game by Marvin Glass and Associates is dated 1966, later it was produced by Mattel. Next to the bean bag where Halliday child is sitting there are also the **DC Comics comics of Superman**. The TV cabinet contains recorded **VHS** and also the original one of **Inner Space**. Above the TV there is a rubber puppet with the features of the **Godzilla Monster King**. On the left of Halliday the child, on the floor, there are maps of the role-playing game **of Dungeons & Dragons**.

When Halliday sits down, he has a desk in front of the **electronic game *Etch A Sketch***. Instead, when you kneel to look for the egg you can see on the desk next to the TV a **KC3 Analog Joystick** of the 1990 NIB for Apple / IBM and next to a model of a **Hotwheels**. Leaning on the right side of this desk, there is the box containing the game *Computer Battleship*, electronic game of the **Naval Battle** created by MB in 1980. Behind Halliday there is a **Commodore 64**. Home Computers manufactured by Commodore Business Machines Inc 1982. There is a **floppy disk reader** for Commodore 64 and Commodore 128 released in the mid-80s, its code is *Commodore 1570*. Near it there is an *Intellivision* **console** made by Mattel Electronics in 1979. At a certain point Halliday picks up the *Lost in Space Robot B9* **toy**. While holding the egg behind you can see: a **5¼-inch floppy disk, magnetic** media used by many computers of that time including the Commodore 1570 and a **model** toy of a *Porsche Carrera* on it.

When Parzival is framed with the egg in his hands, and Halliday is coming out of the door, to his right is a low bookcase with a series of books and magazines. Among these we can see the **Lost in Space B9 robot**, some toy cars, a pair of **yellow dice** with black numbers called *Fuzzy Dice* that are mainly used for cars, some rubber dinosaurs, some games, and a **box** containing a set of rackets ping pong, net and balls or *Spear's Champion Table Tennis*. In the bookcase to the left of the door we distinguish two **books**. The first one on the first shelf above, is the *Guinness Book of Records in 1987*. The second, on the third shelf starting from the top, is the novel *Koko* written by Peter Straub. This is an American writer known for his fantastic and horror works. Koko is considered the novel of his return, after four years of absence, to write and treats in a crude and terrifying way the Vietnam War. Straub is an old friend of Stephen King with whom he has also worked professionally.

Poster

Halliday's room is full of prints, including posters, postcards, flyers, and banners. There are some depicting video games and others related to movies. Below you will find the lists of prints divided by section. To help you to identify where these are in the room, we have divided it into four zones, where each of these is identified with a wall. That the one of the door, the one entering to the left of the door and the one entering to the right.

Videogiochi

On the right wall we have: the horizontal poster of Joust, the poster of **The Legend of Zelda A Link to the Past** in the Japanese version, the flyer of **Pac-Man** version for console Atari VCS 2600, the flyer of **Donkey Kong** of Nintendo (1980), the flyer of **Gyruss** shot'em made by Konami in 1983, the poster is the version for Nintendo, two **postcards** of *Xevious* that are part of a series of six. On the left wall (attached to the sloping wall at the back of the room) there is another *Xevious* post **card** and the *Black Tiger* **poster**. Also on the door is the *Dungeons & Dragons Red Dragon* poster.

Movie

On the left wall there are the **posters** of *Dark Crystal, Breakfast Club* and *Real Genius* comedy (1985), directed by Martha Coolidge and played by a young Val Kilmer. There are also the posters of **_Excalibur, Raiders of the Lost Ark, and Lady Hawk_**. The **poster** of the movie **_The Revenge of the Nerds_** can be glimpsed in the sloping part at the top.

Music

On the wall on the left there is the **Album cover** of the **_Devo_** Freedom of Choise, the LP of the soundtrack by **_Wargames_** and the LP of the album **_2112_** of the **_Rush_** of which we also find the poster.

Halliday scene exit

Halliday's final phrase "Thanks for playing my game" is a reference to **Super Mario 64** videogame for Nintendo, that when it was finished, Mario, at the end of the credits, thanked the player for playing.

End of the journey

When Samantha and Wade are interrupted by the lawyers, they open the doors of the van showing on the right of the screen the **sticker** of the movie **Moon on the moon** by George Melies (1902). When Helen closes the back of the van we can see, on the left , a **sticker** of the famous pirate skull *Jolly Roger.*

Wade's room

When the kids can finally rest and even think about being together, we find ourselves in Wade's room. In the first frame, on the right wall, you can see two cabinets: one is from the **game *Space Invaders*** and the other from ***Robotron 2084***. In the first shelving of the library, starting from the bottom left, there are four mini arcades. Starting from the right there is the **handheld game** of *Scramble*, version with the red writing, of **Grandmaster** (1980), next to that of ***Frogger*** produced by Gakken in 1982 there's another pac-man handheld game like the one we saw in Halliday's morgue at the beginning of the movie and above the green one is ***Safari*** made by the company "Bambino" in 1981. Still on the right we can see the giant of the alien portrayed in the ***Space Invaders*** cabinet. On the window there is the **poster** of the first **Star Trek** movie (1966); Below is the framed **poster** of the **Black Tiger** videogame. On the left side, on the ground, there is a **Colecovsion** console. When the shot moves to where Wade and Samantha are, in the background we can see a pinball, the **Revenge from Mars** created by Midway in 1999. While in the foreground (hanging on the pillar) there is a 1:1 scale reproduction of the ***Excalibur sword*** that Parzival wears as a patch on the denim jacket. We also see an arcade cocktail by **Joust**. On your left is ***Robby The Robot*** in 1: 1 scale, in the lower corner a reproduction of ***R2-D2***, the droid of the Star Wars saga. In front of the window you can admire the double blade ***Klingonian Bat'leth***. This is a **weapon** of the

Klingons, the aliens of the Star Trek television and movie series. To the right of the Klingonian Bat'leth is the ***Sharp GF-7600 Radio Cassette Boombox*** (1980) which Parzival uses in the final battle and which, as we have written, is a reference to the movie Say anything... On the table in front of the sofa there is a **Nintendo Entertainment System (NES)** and a **Sony Betamax SL-C7** videorecorder (1981); above it there is a SEGA **Master System 2** console.

Ending

And here we are, the adventure of the Unofficial Guide to Ready Player One easter eggs is over. During these months of work we have discovered more and more references hidden in the movie and we have brought them to the light as if they were treasures, we have seen them, watched, observed, and studied. Then we wrote them in the pages of this book sure to give you something precious, and each time we admired the work of Steven Spielberg and his team, composed of people who have decided what to insert and where; thinking about how much the object should be visible. The treasures that we brought to the light are part of a period that is very dear to us, a period in which we grew up and that made us who we are.